ANGER MANAGEMENT FOR PARENTS

MANAGE ANGER WITH LOVE, HEAL TRIGGERS & RAISE CONFIDENT, CARING CHILDREN. YOUR BRAIN PLASTICITY AND QUANTUM TOOLS BUILD EMOTIONAL INTELLIGENCE IN HAPPY RELATIONSHIPS

HADLEY FINCH

CONTENTS

INTRODUCTION

You're racing through the morning. Maybe you're trying to get shoes on a toddler who thinks socks are for chewing, or you're reminding your teenager for the third time to put their phone away at breakfast. Your coffee has gone cold. You hear yourself shout. Suddenly, you see your child tense up. Your heart sinks. For a split second, you wish that you could hit rewind.

If this sounds familiar, please know you're not alone. Parenting can feel like a pressure cooker. The small stresses pile up. Spilled milk, lost homework, a sibling squabble can explode into yelling. Some days, it takes all you have to stay calm. On other days, you blow off steam. Guilt sweeps in like a tidal wave.

I saw these cycles as I grew up in a home where one parent's anger could turn a peaceful moment into something tense and scary. I saw how joy could vanish in an instant, replaced by a distressing silence that follows shouting. My memories of my parent with unhealed anger issues don't include their quiet moments of keeping us nourished in a lovely home. My dominant memories are of that parent's loud, uncontrolled raging, echoing in my body for years. I've since learned about the brain's "**Negativity Bias**," which hardwires threats into long-term memory storage to protect us from harm. In contrast, positive experiences quickly fade, unless they're reinforced consistently with loving kindness. (see APA list: 82, 83, 84)

Exploring the science helped me understand why one parent's angry outbursts and excessive discipline gave me a short fuse and shaped how I related to anger as a parent and partner. I carried old stress into adulthood, often wondering why one small thing could make me swear like that angry parent did. The science showed me that one parent's short temper and tendency to swear were contagious, and I caught them.

I learned why the brain can easily become stuck in negative loops at the mere sound of a parent yelling. I learned how to calm my inherited temper and release my inherited stress with the holistic toolkit I share with you here. I learned how to recognize childhood trauma, heal it as an adult, and break the cycle of intergenerational anger to spare my children from harm. I wrote this book because I want to walk beside you as you do this work, too.

I'm Hadley Finch. In my past work as a radio host and author, known as America's Love Guide, I devoted over a decade to teaching skills that help people transition from a brain state of survival to thriving in life and relationships. My teaching and communications degree from Northwestern University equipped me with the tools to inspire the best in others, while my own life gave me the motivation to look deeper. I know the science and the heart of these struggles. I know the joyful relief that comes from using expert tools to transform conflict into connection, helping release the grip of a parent's anger that's stored in a child's body.

This book is for you, the busy parent who sometimes feels overwhelmed and seeks practical tools to make a change. You'll explore proven techniques, drawn from both research and real-life experience, that you can use right away to help you understand your emotional triggers, manage your reactions in a way that your brain accepts rather than resists, and care for yourself—so you can raise confident, caring, emotionally intelligent children in a happy relationship.

You'll start by learning how to identify the patterns that trigger your reactions. You'll learn how to calm your body and mind, even during a conflict. You'll see why self-care isn't selfish or a luxury. It's a lifeline in your busy life.

You'll practice responding to your child's big feelings without being swept up in their emotions. You'll help your child's brain recover from the chronic stress of being exposed to yelling, negativity, criticism, and even harsh discipline if you're delivering it.

You'll learn why a child's five basic needs must be met to motivate them to fulfill their potential, and how a parent's unchecked anger hinders this.

You'll also see how your thoughts shape your reactions. Cognitive Behavioral Techniques (CBT) can uncover stories you may tell yourself. You'll challenge stories like "I'm failing as a parent" or "My child is doing this on purpose" and rewrite them. You'll see how a slight shift in your thinking can change everything, from the words you say to the way you (and your child) feel inside.

You'll discover practical strategies for parents of toddlers, pre-teens, and teenagers. Each chapter offers exercises to manage hot-button issues at each stage, such as when your toddler throws a tantrum on the plane, when your pre-teen slams a door on you, or when your teenager gives you the silent treatment. Each exercise is rooted in solid research and the latest brain science you can trust.

I want you to feel seen and supported throughout your journey to manage anger with love and be the parent (and the partner) you want to be now. That's why you'll engage in quizzes, self-assessment tools, and exercises in every chapter. They aren't just for fun, though I hope you enjoy them. They help you track your progress, measure your growth, replace old habits with better ones, and tailor the tools to fit your family's changing needs.

I'll share real-life stories and less-than-perfect moments from parents. We'll discuss the times we've snapped, the guilt that follows, and the ways we can laugh, learn, and forgive ourselves to foster growth. No one always gets this right, so there is no judgment here. You'll find honesty, empathy, and much-needed lightness as you start celebrating small wins that lead to the lasting change you desire.

Have you ever wished for more peace in your home, fewer arguments, and more connection? Excellent. You're in the right place. This workbook helps you see conflict as an opportunity for deeper understanding.

You will understand that you've done nothing wrong. You've been doing your best with the information you've had thus far. And now that you're here, your best will get better every day, in every way, as you learn to model emotional intelligence for your child and teach them, by example, how to form happy relationships.

There's no need to be a perfect parent. You only need to be willing to grow. These tools help you manage your anger with love and help your children become more resilient, caring, and confident. Together, you can transform challenging moments into chances for more joyful interactions with fewer fights.

CHAPTER 1
UNDERSTANDING PARENTAL ANGER AND WHAT TRIGGERS YOU

SOME MORNINGS BEGIN with good intentions, a gentle voice, patience, and a hot cup of coffee. Then juice spills on homework, a work emergency pops up, and your toddler screams louder than a foghorn. Suddenly, your jaw clenches. Then regretful words spill out before you can stop them. Have you ever asked yourself, "Why am I so quick to snap?" "Where does all this anger come from?" Wonderful. This means you are already moving toward change by being curious about how anger signals where positive shifts are needed.

Anger is part of parenting and being human. Research indicates that approximately 70% of parents experience anger toward their children at times, and nearly half feel irritation or anger at least once a week (APA List: Source 2).

You're not alone or broken. However, unchecked anger can leave lasting scars on loved ones. How do you prevent this? A vital first step is to understand what is going on beneath the surface before you can change your reactions to triggers and reset relationship hot buttons.

THE ANATOMY OF PARENTAL ANGER: WHAT TRIGGERS YOU?

Anger isn't just an isolated emotion. It's a full-body response. When you feel threatened, disrespected, or overwhelmed, it activates your brain's alarm system. The amygdala, deep in your brain, flashes a warning. Our ancestors needed this to survive. Now, that same warning system is set off when your teenager rolls their eyes or your partner questions your parenting. Your heart races. Muscles in your shoulders, jaw, and neck are tense. A headache might start. All of this can happen in seconds before a single word is spoken.

Parental anger is often triggered by small, everyday events that accumulate over time. Identifying what sets you off as a parent isn't always obvious. At first, you only see the explosion -- a thrown saucer, a sharp reply, or the urge to walk away -- without realizing what sparked it. How do you bring the sparks into focus? By pausing and looking for patterns.

Your history matters more than you might think. Pause and consider how discipline looked when you were a child. Were raised voices and swearing common? Did anyone take the time to hear your side of the story? Or did you learn to swallow your feelings that something is wrong, because you were harshly punished when you expressed them?

Parenting styles from long ago often echo in the present. If you bristle at a child's backtalk or freeze up when conflict arises, these reactions may come from old wounds. It's not a reason to blame your parents. It's an opportunity to see how your early years have shaped your responses today.

What if your teenager's sarcastic shout provokes words you vowed never to say? Your child's shout may pour salt on your old emotional wounds. The mere sound of shouting or criticism can revive feelings from growing up in a harsh environment, wiring your brain to expect threats. This triggers the fight-or-flight response, even if no real danger exists. If left unhealed, childhood trauma can have a lifelong impact on your nervous system.

Stress is a stealthy trigger. The pressures of work, financial worries, deadlines, and dozens of tasks you juggle every day all build up. When stress builds, patience thins. You're more likely to react sharply after a poor night's sleep. Back-to-back nights with children waking up can turn even a minor annoyance into a meltdown. Overdoing caffeine to stay alert or reaching for a quick ultra-processed snack can also leave you jittery and short-tempered. Alcohol may numb stress for a moment, yet it often leaves you less able to respond calmly.

What else makes irritability more likely? Your energy stagnates when you don't move your body or spend time outdoors. When creative outlets vanish and meaningful connections wane, anger slips into those gaps. You may not notice how much you need a walk in the park or five quiet minutes until your toddler asks "Why" for the tenth time, making you want to scream.

Unattended hurt leads to anger. You may notice that anger flares when you aren't meeting your needs, such as wanting time to yourself or feeling appreciated. When your expectations clash with reality (wanting a peaceful bedtime but getting chaos), your anger can fill the gap between hope and disappointment.

Can this pattern be changed? Yes, you can change a pattern once you identify it through emotional awareness. This means paying attention to your anger and what triggers it. Was it exhaustion? Feeling dismissed? One demand too many? Let's explore a trusted tool that identifies your triggers and the patterns that activate them.

INCREASE EMOTIONAL AWARENESS EXERCISE:

Start Your Journal of Anger Triggers. Try this for one week: First, choose a notebook or an online note service and label it, **Manage Anger With Love Journal.** List your first category: My Anger Triggers. Jot down details of each moment when anger arises this week. What happened just before? What thoughts came to mind? What feelings? The act of writing untangles what's swirling in your mind.

Keep your journal nearby so you can note the anger scenarios that keep showing up in your daily life and the early physical signs that indicate you're being triggered.

Create a List of Frequent Conflicts. Include who was involved, what time it happened, even what you had eaten before it, and how much sleep you got. This reveals patterns that are easy to miss in the buzz of family life. You aren't creating a journal of complaints. You are shining a light on the situations that leave you angry and frustrated again and again.

Understanding the anatomy of anger—how it lives in your body and mind — isn't about blaming or shaming yourself or your child. It's about building self-awareness for real change. As you recognize anger cues, you may pause and choose a different response.

A fundamental transformation begins by facing anger with curiosity and compassion, rather than denying it or running from it. You will be guided through each step of this transformative process right after you gain a deeper understanding of how unhealed anger impacts you and your entire family.

THE EMOTIONAL DOMINO: HOW ANGER AFFECTS FAMILY DYNAMICS

When anger enters a home, it moves fast. Like a domino that topples the next, it doesn't stop at one person. You might not even realize it, but a single angry outburst can send shock waves through every member of your family. One harsh word or slammed door can fuel sibling squabbles, silent tension with your partner, and a sense of unease that lingers long after the moment passes.

Children soak up this emotional charge. They might start snapping at each other, compete for attention, or withdraw into their own worlds. The youngest child may cry or cling to you, while older ones might roll their eyes or retreat to their rooms.

Partners respond, too, with defensiveness and more conflict or by shutting down and avoiding you altogether. Does yelling ever make your partner feel closer to you? Or does it repel them? Does yelling ever produce the effect you want?

Do you notice less connection with your partner and more bickering between your children after you lose your temper? This is the ripple effect of angry outbursts. This powerful phenomenon is known as **"Emotional Contagion."**

Think of it as the way moods jump from person to person, like an airborne virus. When you walk into a room where someone is laughing, it's hard not to smile. The same goes for anger. Raised voices and tense faces can instantly shift the energy in a home.

Children are exceptionally skilled at picking up emotional cues. If they see you yell or storm out of a room, they absorb your tension. They may release it later, perhaps by yelling at a sibling, throwing toys, or talking back. Even if a child doesn't show it right away, internal pressures can build up over time, as they mirror your moods and behaviors.

An angry morning can shape the day for everyone. Children go to school on edge. You feel stressed at work. Homecoming is tense instead of warm. This cycle doesn't just shape today. It sets the blueprint for tomorrow.

A child who sees calm conflict resolution learns to pause and talk things through. A child who sees a parent handle anger through shouting or withdrawal learns to believe this is how conflict is typically resolved. Some children mimic what they see, growing quick to anger. Others become anxious or fearful, always bracing for the next outburst.

What does the brain science say? Studies show that exposure to frequent parental anger can shrink the hippocampus of a child's brain, which limits their ability to learn, focus, regulate emotion, and feel safe.

A child exposed to frequent outbursts absorbs chaos instead of calm, keeping their brain in a state of high alert. If you notice that your child is getting stuck in negative moods, consider what emotional patterns they're seeing at home. (see APA list: 46)

Here's the good news. Patterns can be changed. Recognizing how anger moves through a family is the first step toward stopping its spread.

CHANGE FAMILY PATTERNS EXERCISE

A Simple Yet Powerful Practice That Can Change Patterns Is A Family Emotional Check-in. Set aside a few minutes after dinner or before bed. Ask everyone how they're feeling. The goal isn't to fix it but to create a space where feelings are named and heard without judgment. When interacting with a young child, use simple words like happy, excited, sad, mad, and scared. Older children and adults can grasp emotional nuances and share more details.

What are the benefits of emotional check-ins? You teach a child that it's okay to feel mad or frustrated. You demonstrate how to handle those feelings without escalating into rage that harms others. Over time, new patterns take root. Your presence spreads calm (like anger once disturbed) through words, actions, and understanding. Each step forward ripples outward, giving your family a fresh start day after day.

Increasing awareness is like building muscle. It grows with practice and attention. Your mindful awareness creates a small space between what happens and how you respond.

DO WHAT WORKS AND AVOID WHAT DOESN'T WITH SELF-REFLECTION EXERCISES

How do you track what works and what doesn't? Check in with yourself often as you explore our Self-Reflection Tools and Exercises:

Doing "The Work" by Byron Katie can cut through spiraling thoughts that provoke angry outbursts. Ask yourself four liberating questions about a recurring thought: Is it true? Can I be certain that it's true? How do

I react when I believe that thought? How would I act without that thought? Answering these four questions honestly can slow reactivity and invite curiosity that promotes understanding instead of anger or blame.

Writing "Morning Pages," inspired by Julia Cameron, is a valuable start to your day. Set aside ten minutes after waking to write three pages by hand. No editing. No rules. Write whatever comes up. Keep writing without thinking, writing gibberish if necessary to keep your pen moving on the page for 10 to 20 minutes. This practice uncovers buried frustration and clears it from the windshield of your mind before it colors your day. Clearing thought debris reveals a clear view of the day's possibilities.

Keep your morning pages for your eyes only, so you can discard your mental debris on the page without snooping eyes on it.

Besides clearing my thought debris, I began writing lyrics for an album of songs in my daily morning pages. This helped me channel insights I gained on my journey from lost love to the fire of love into a soulful pop-country-bluegrass album theme I call **Soulgrass**. (Listen to this album on my blog: HappySexyLove.com Click: Love Songs) Once you clear your frustrating mental debris by writing morning pages, imagine the possibilities you will see in each day.

Noticing "Glimmers" begins disarming your triggers. Glimmers (a term coined by polyvagal therapist Deb Dana) are flashes of joy and awe that tell you all is well, like sunlight on your kitchen table, laughter from the next room, or a kind text from a friend.

Seeing glimmers of awe and quiet joy helps your brain shift out of a fight-or-flight survival mode and into a calm, thriving mode. This isn't a one-and-done exercise. Reflecting on what brings you joy is an ongoing act of care for yourself and your family.

Alternatively, each time you pause to notice what choices irritate you or push your buttons, you give yourself a chance to choose differently next time. Weeks and months of making these small shifts can accumulate into real change. Your children will notice a new lightness in you, even if they can't put it into words yet.

The gift of self-reflection keeps on giving as you choose your best response to anger triggers that are activated in parenting and partnering.

UNDERSTAND THE GUILT CYCLE OF PARENTAL REGRET

After an angry outburst, shame, regret, and guilt may settle in. This cycle of anger followed by guilt can feel endless. It starts when a daily frustration sparks an angry outburst. Afterward, you may replay the moment in your mind, wishing you could take it back. Remorse doesn't sit quietly. It gnaws at your confidence as a parent. It whispers that you're failing or causing harm.

That inner voice grows louder if you grew up in a home where discipline meant yelling, shaming, or delivering physical punishment. You promised yourself things would be different. Yet, in the heat of the moment, old patterns creep in. You may watch yourself repeat them and then regret it.

Guilt has a sneaky way of steering how you parent. One day, you might overcorrect, swinging from anger to leniency, letting your child get away with things to soothe your regret. You might find yourself saying "Yes" to things you'd usually refuse or showering your child with treats as a way to make up for harsh words. The next day, you might come down harder on minor mistakes, echoing the strictness you endured as a child.

This inconsistency leaves a child confused about discipline and boundaries. They wonder which version of you they'll meet each day. Are you the parent who lets everything slide? Or the one who explodes over socks left on the floor? Over time, this back-and-forth erodes authority, trust, and emotional safety.

Sometimes, guilt takes a dangerous turn. It tempts us to justify our anger as necessary or even noble by labeling it "**Sacred Anger**" and by convincing ourselves that a child needs to learn harsh lessons early. Yet, deep down, most parents know when anger crosses into territory that causes harm. Screaming or using physical force instills fear and fosters rage, rather than respect and love. It leaves invisible, lasting bruises on a child's heart and nervous system.

It's easy to repeat what we experienced as a child because it feels familiar. Yet familiarity doesn't mean it's proper or healthy. When we normalize rage or justify repeated outbursts as sacred anger, we miss an opportunity to understand the message of rage and foster safer, stronger bonds with a child.

What if you were slapped, spanked, or beaten as a child? Did you ever wonder if your parents questioned their corporal punishment strategy that inflicted pain and stirred your hostility against them?

ASK WHETHER IT'S NOBLER TO BEAT OR NOT TO BEAT YOUR CHILD. THAT IS THE QUESTION. WHAT'S THE SCIENCE-BACKED ANSWER?

The saying, **Spare The Rod, Spoil The Child,** does not directly appear in the Bible as many believe. It was coined by the English writer Samuel Butler in 1662, when parents interpreted the "rod" as an instrument to beat their children to keep them on the right path. How does this violent view contradict the rod's metaphorical meaning?

In biblical times, the shepherd's "rod" was used for guiding and protecting the sheep, not for beating them. It was used to keep the sheep on the right path and to fend off predators. In this context, the rod symbolizes the loving, guiding hand of a parent who protects a child from danger and wayward paths.

The rod can represent knowledge, because consistent guidance and moral training are a core part of the biblical concept of discipline. Applied to parenting, sparing the rod, or withholding guidance and discipline, can be framed as failing to be a loving guide for your child, leaving them unprepared for life. (see APA list: 81)

When were parents asked to reconsider their view of "Sparing the rod"? In 1946, **Dr. Benjamin Spock's The Common Sense Book of Baby and Child Care** challenged the conventional wisdom that "Spare the rod, spoil the child" instructs parents to use corporal punishment to keep children on the right path.

That went from being a time-honored truth to being a taboo, labeled as child abuse in the decades after Doctor Spock first advocated for a more compassionate approach. Subsequent research findings have supported the use of positive discipline by parents and warned about the significant harm caused by inflicting the pain of corporal punishment on children.

What does the latest science say? Numerous studies consistently report that the pain and coercive force of physical punishment elicit a child's aggression and antisocial behavior.

As a recipient of corporal punishment from early childhood until I grew strong enough to protect myself, I attest that physical punishment triggered anger, which intensified into hate of the parent who kept inflicting painful punishments (as they had been punished as a child). My childhood anger and hate were endlessly renewable energies, renewing with each belting and each threat or memory of one.

Do you know any two, four, six, or eight-year-old child who deserves a belt whipping or any other form of physical punishment? This trauma lingers in a child's body, triggering not only anger and hate but also an excessive reaction to the pain of the slightest injury as an adult, in my experience.

CONSIDER HOW SCIENTIFIC EVIDENCE IMPACTS A BELIEF THAT PHYSICAL PUNISHMENT IMPROVES BEHAVIOR

In the 1990s, Neuroimaging studies revealed that physical punishment of children can reduce the brain's gray matter, potentially lowering IQ. It can also alter the brain's dopaminergic regions associated with vulnerability to the abuse of drugs and alcohol.

Decades of studies have shown the negative impact of physical punishment on a child's neurological, cognitive, emotional, and social development, as well as their physical health. A survey of research conducted over the past few decades reveals that no study has found physical punishment to have a long-term positive effect. In contrast, most studies have reported negative effects. (see APA list: 81)

Global governments have responded to these clinical findings. As of year-end 2025, the physical punishment of a child has been outlawed in 68 countries. The United States still allows physical punishment in the home (where child and spousal abuse typically take place).

The Future Is Non-Violent Parenting. There is considerable evidence that parents who learn to observe their child's behavior, communicate clearly, and apply contingent consequences experience positive effects on both their own psychological well-being and their child's behavior and mental health.

I'm thankful that for decades I've explored how to break an intergenerational cycle of corporal punishment, release its stored trauma, and protect my children from harm, using the holistic and quantum tools that I'm sharing with you here. Growing through this pain, finding lessons in it, and sharing the path out of it have also helped me transform the energy of anger into love and gratitude.

What's the way out of the cycle that triggers anger? It's not perfection but self-compassion. Being gentle with yourself after a regretful action is revolutionary. You prevent guilt from spiraling into self-loathing or denial when you pause and notice what happened. "I lost my temper. I wish I hadn't yelled."

Accepting full responsibility without self-attack makes it possible to recognize the plea for change that anger presents. Setting realistic expectations for yourself is crucial. No parent is always calm. You're human, wired for big emotion and stretched thinly by demands.

What do you do when anger erupts and triggers guilt? Guilt can point the way toward positive change when you use it as a vital source of information. How? Ask yourself: What did I need at that moment? Was I tired, hungry, or feeling unappreciated? Was I repeating words that were hurled at me long ago? Was my anger trying to protect me from harm?

Anger often highlights areas in your life that require healing or support. Is it time for more rest, help from your partner, or a break from unrealistic standards? What actions would help you meet your needs? Will you take those actions to help yourself feel better and do better each day? Will you list these actions on your daily calendar as a reminder?

Author Maya Angelo said, "We do better when we know better." Now you are better informed about the harm that unchecked anger can inflict on your loved ones, and the ways you can manage anger with love, including self-love.

How do you ensure that doing your best gets better every day, in every way? The techniques and exercises that you explore here will work for you when you put them into practice. Science says that practice makes permanent.

REPAIR RELATIONSHIPS AFTER AN ANGRY OUTBURST: TECHNIQUES

What's a best practice in repairing a relationship after an angry outburst? Choose the techniques that feel right for you among several options:

Consider apologizing, revealing your vulnerability, accepting total responsibility, and even requesting your family's patient support as you rebuild trust day after day. Are you willing to list your favorite techniques on your calendar as a reminder to practice them?

Children can be incredibly forgiving when a parent honestly owns up to missteps. Sit with your child after an outburst. Offer an apology that goes beyond "I'm sorry." Explain what happened beneath the surface. "I was upset and raised my voice. That wasn't fair to you. I'm sorry." Let them see that grown-ups can struggle with feelings and still take responsibility for their actions.

You might ask your child (and your partner) to be patient with you while you work to break the habit of saying or doing harsh things that may mirror what you faced as a child. You might even give your family permission to hold up their hand as a stop sign, or to say "Breathe" or "Pause" during your outburst, as a helpful reminder. Your honest, consistent effort to heal triggers and manage anger with love builds trust day after day.

Remember that old family patterns do not trap you. Each time you apologize and try again, you teach your child that everyone is capable of growth and forgiveness. You build an empowering legacy by creating a home where regrettable actions are met with understanding rather than rage, where love and warmth can survive difficult times and thrive.

WHY DOES A PARENT WITH UNHEALED ANGER NEED TO KNOW THE HIERARCHY OF A CHILD'S TOP FIVE NEEDS?

The patterns you establish as a parent are best designed to help satisfy your child's five basic needs, so they are motivated to fulfill their potential. Unchecked anger interferes with this process.

In 1943, Psychologist Abraham Maslow argued in his hierarchy of human needs, later depicted as a five-level pyramid, that the foundational needs at the base of the pyramid ideally should be satisfied before a child can attend to the next level of needs, ultimately reaching the peak of the pyramid.

This means that parents are wise to help fulfill their child's basic physiological needs for food, shelter, and clothing, which is the foundation of the pyramid. Above that, a parent fulfills a child's need for safety. Above that is a child's need for love and belonging. Once those basic needs are met (the sequence may vary), a child will feel motivated to attend to their higher need for self-esteem. Finally, at the peak of Maslow's pyramid lies the need for self-actualization, which is fulfilled by being the best you that you can be. (see APA List: 57)

LEARN HOW UNCHECKED ANGER IMPACTS A PARENT'S ABILITY TO FULFILL A CHILD'S FIVE BASIC NEEDS

Anger and Your Child's Development: A Critical Look

Children are like sponges, soaking up the tone of your voice, the look in your eyes, and the energy you bring into a room. When anger flares regularly at home, it leaves more than a temporary mark. It can shape how your child sees themself and the world around them. You may notice that your child hesitates to trust new friends or teachers, or holds back in situations where openness would be beneficial.

Some children respond to anger by shutting down emotionally, becoming quiet, withdrawn, or anxious. Others might go the opposite direction, acting out with defiant words or risky behavior to regain some sense of control. These aren't personality quirks. They may be adaptive shields against the emotional storms that blow up without warning and shatter a child's sense of safety.

Consider Experimental Evidence Of How Words & Intentions Affect Us

In Dr. Masaru Emoto's 1994 experiments, he provided photographic images showing water exposed to positive words, such as "love" and "thank you," and uplifting music formed lovely, symmetrical ice crystals. Water subjected to negative words, such as "hate", "fool", and "anger", and discordant, jarring music, formed distorted, jagged ice crystals.

Dr. Emoto's findings are particularly relevant to our bodies, which are primarily composed of water.

What does the science say? The messages we convey through our voice, touch, and presence have a profound impact on the recipient at a cellular level. A child who hears calm encouragement feels safe and valued. A child who hears angry outbursts absorbs tension that can linger for years. The science might sound poetic, yet it underscores a simple truth: A child's emotional landscape is shaped by what parents (and teachers, caregivers, and coaches) pour into it. (APA list: 4)

What kind of ice crystals would form if Dr. Emoto's experiments had included a recent term, "Toxic Masculinity", which says that all males are bad and violent animals?

The words attributed to males, including "toxic", "violent", and "bad", fall into the category of negative words and harmful intentions that Dr. Emoto claimed produced jagged, chaotic ice crystals.

Dr. Emoto's experiments were criticized in the scientific community for lacking control groups and for suggesting that human consciousness can alter the molecular structure of water. Yet, Dr. Emoto's 1994 experiments may have inspired future researchers who have scientifically verified the related phenomenon known as **Emotional Contagion**, demonstrating the spontaneous synchronization of emotions among individuals.

Scientific evidence now shows that people can transfer positive and negative moods and feelings to family members, groups, and even entire social networks, without any physical interaction. (see ASA list: 71)

Experimental evidence of massive-scale emotional contagion was documented in **Facebook's 2012 experiment** on nearly 700,000 users. When Facebook secretly reduced the visibility of positive emotional posts, users posted more negative content, and vice versa. This demonstrates that emotional states can spread through online social networks without direct contact.

Although Facebook's ethics were criticized for conducting this research without first obtaining its users' informed consent, Facebook's research findings on emotional contagion have not been disputed. (see APA list: 72)

EXPLORE HOW THE EMOTIONAL CONTAGION OF TOXIC MASCULINITY IMPACTS BOYS AND MEN. EMBRACE THE ANTIDOTES

The negative term, Toxic Masculinity, is causing harm and fueling rage in boys and men, according to the mental health experts who were quoted in a 9-22-25 article in the **Wall Street Journal**. (see APA list: 70)

The gist of the article asserts that a boy knows in his heart what it means to be a good man. Yet his heartfelt knowledge creates an inner conflict when dealing with the distorted notion of toxic masculinity that is being taught, triggering anger in boys and men and leading to violent behavior in some males.

"They already think I'm violent, so I'll be violent." That's how the false prophecy of toxic masculinity can influence thoughts and behavior, so it becomes true.

How do you embrace the antidote? Parents can practice using our science-backed techniques to release the anger and trauma triggered by this prophecy's assault on every fiber of the masculine being, and reclaim their productive power. Parents also can teach age-appropriate strategies to their children. In some cases, a therapist may be needed to support the treatment of chronic anger, helping create a sense of safety that defuses rage.

Each male child (and female child) needs to hear consistent, calm encouragement that brings out their best. Receiving this encouragement from parents, caregivers, teachers, and coaches helps a child feel safe and valued, ensuring that a false notion like toxic masculinity doesn't influence behavior and cause harm.

Have you ever wondered why you self-sabotage or feel so frustrated with yourself? If you make choices that "blow up your life," you may be stuck with false beliefs about yourself that arose from messages you heard as a child. How do you get unstuck? The first step is to create awareness.

IDENTIFY THE MESSAGES THAT FORMED YOUR BELIEFS EXERCISE

In your **Manage Anger With Love Journal,** add a new Category: **My Self-Fulfilling Prophecies.** Jot down messages you heard while growing up. List the feelings, beliefs, actions, and results that each negative message triggered and each positive message inspired.

Consider these messages: "You're a born leader." "You're the smartest kid I know." "You can do it." "You're going to change the world." "I love all the wonders of you."

Did you hear messages like these, that make you smile and lift moods? List the good-mood messages and how they affected your beliefs and your actions in your childhood, and today. What else did you want to hear? Jot that down.

Consider these messages: "You're a dumb loser." "You always make stupid mistakes." "You're a mean jerk." "You're too bossy." "You ruin everything."

Did you hear messages like these, that make you cringe and put you in a bad mood? List the bad-mood messages and how they affected your beliefs and your actions in your childhood, and today. What did you want to hear instead? Jot that down.

What messages are you telling your child? Jot them down, too. Imagine what your child wants to hear instead. If you say that, how might your child respond? Will you say it and see what changes? Jot that down, too.

This exercise reveals how the messages you hear about yourself can shape your feelings, beliefs, behavior, and how people respond to you. This also applies to the messages that you tell your child (and your partner).

This exercise also uncovers what messages can be getting in your way and your child's way. Identifying a limiting, false belief is the first step in the process that releases it and replaces it with a productive truth, helping you reclaim your authentic, productive power.

How do you reclaim your power as you begin to manage anger with love? You will start handling frustration more effectively by taking a deep breath and expressing your needs without yelling or lashing out. This gives your child a script for managing their frustrating moments. You teach, by example, that it's possible to feel mad or disappointed without losing control.

You can give your child words for their big feelings. "I'm frustrated because my tower fell." "I feel angry you won't play with me." Help them name and acknowledge their emotions instead of suppressing or acting them out. When you show a child how to express what hurts or scares them, you give them an effective tool that helps build happy relationships at every stage of life.

You gain more incentive to disarm your anger triggers once you understand that your child's exposure to angry outbursts can create anxiety and lower their self-esteem.

Children who grow up around shouting or criticism may develop internal scripts, such as "I'm not good enough," "Everything is my fault," or "If I try to speak up, I'll get in trouble." Some children become chronic pleasers, constantly seeking approval or walking on eggshells. Others adopt negative self-talk, falsely blaming themselves for being the cause of their parents' worst days. How does a parent help rectify this?

Let Shift Happen. Trust that you can start a shift by teaching problem-solving skills. When something goes wrong, invite your child to brainstorm solutions with you. "What could we do differently next time?" Encourage open communication where honesty is met with warmth instead of judgment.

You model kind-hearted truth-telling to inspire openness and trust in your family. You make expressing gratitude part of your routine. Perhaps you give thanks out loud for small wins and good times in each day. At bedtime, talk together about what went well, what was tough that day, and what you might do better tomorrow.

The home you build with your words, actions, and responses becomes the blueprint for how your child will navigate the world, treat others, and see themselves when things don't go as planned.

What if anger has cast long shadows in your family? Every new day offers another chance to flood those shadows with the light of loving kindness and understanding. Doing this daily is a neural investment that rewires your brain and your child's brain from a state of survival-mode reactivity into a calm, reflective, and connected state in which love thrives. You can't banish anger forever. You can ensure that loving kindness always prevails.

You are being guided through that process now, so you can consistently be the parent (and the partner) you want to be.

CHAPTER 2
BUILDING EMOTIONAL INTELLIGENCE AND EMPATHY IN PARENTING

IMAGINE STANDING in a noisy living room. The TV is loud. Children argue over the remote. Your phone pings with work messages. You feel your stress rise. Yet, instead of snapping, you pause and take a breath. You understand your frustration, choose your words carefully, and then settle the dispute. This isn't magic. It's Emotional Intelligence (EQ) in action.

Emotional Intelligence is the ability to recognize, understand, and manage your own emotions, as well as identify and understand the feelings of others. Emotional intelligence doesn't mean you're always calm. It means you make sense of your feelings, express yourself respectfully, and form strong, healthy bonds with your loved ones, colleagues, and community.

Psychologist and author Daniel Goleman outlines five main pillars of EQ: Self-awareness, Self-regulation, Motivation, Empathy, and Social skills.

Self-awareness means recognizing your emotions as they arise. It means you name stress, anger, and overwhelm before they control your behavior. Your inner radar of self-awareness allows you to pause before reacting.

Self-regulation uses awareness to manage emotions effectively. Instead of yelling or shutting down, you respond more healthily.

Motivation fueled by self-discipline moves you forward despite obstacles.

Empathy bridges you to others as you respond with care for their feelings.

Social skills let you build trust, foster cooperation, and deepen connections. You can listen well, resolve conflicts peacefully, and work together as a team. (See APA list: 1)

Developing these skills transforms your parenting and partnering. You gain the flexibility to sense and prevent conflicts or see them as a chance to deepen emotional connection. This makes family life less tense and more cooperative, even as you face life's toughest challenges.

Developing Emotional Intelligence is a crucial skill set for parents. Why? A high EQ helps you tackle challenges with calm and clarity. Research shows that parents who develop EQ skills tend to have warmer relationships with their children and partners. You're more likely to listen instead of jumping to conclusions. You can set boundaries without guilt and enforce them with calm consistency.

EQ benefits ripple through the whole family. Parents with a high EQ are less likely to spiral into stress because they know how to step back and reset. This steadiness creates a calm environment. Children notice how you handle frustration and learn from you. EQ also strengthens romantic relationships and friendships, giving you more support when parenting feels overwhelming.

Can a high EQ help parents avoid divorce over common issues that include unchecked anger? Yes, according to a Harvard study led by Dr. George Vaillant, who followed 724 married couples for over 30 years. Study findings highlight the significance of emotional coping strategies and the capacity to adapt to life's challenges, which are signs of high EQs. The strongest couples are bonded by facing challenges together as a united team. They choose emotional peace over being right in a fight.

It's not about never fighting, but recovering quickly rather than dwelling on conflicts. The study reveals that emotional intelligence is key. The ability to manage emotions, practice empathy, adapt to challenges, and bounce back from setbacks with resilience is crucial for lasting relationship success and overall happiness. (see APA list: 65, 66, 67)

Can Emotional Intelligence be improved? The good news is you can raise your EQ at any age by the choices you make day after day. Start with honest reflection. How often do I lose my temper? Do I struggle to express my needs? Do I regret how I handle anger, stress, and overwhelm? Your answers are springboards for making productive changes.

TAKE AN EMOTIONAL INTELLIGENCE SELF-ASSESSMENT: HOW'S YOUR EQ?

Try this quick EQ quiz, answering each question with a "Yes" or "No":

1. When I'm upset, I recognize what I'm feeling before reacting.
2. I can calm myself down when angry or stressed.
3. I can see things from my child's (or partner's) perspective.
4. I listen before making assumptions.
5. I can talk about my feelings without placing blame on others.

Give yourself one point for each "Yes." If you score three or fewer, there's room to grow, which is normal.

If you score 4 or 5 "Yes" points, you have a healthy EQ that you may continue to enrich through lifelong self-growth.

This workbook presents tools, techniques, and exercises that help build each pillar of EQ. You can start practicing your favorites now, trusting that repetition makes the results stick. Remember what Science says: "Practice makes permanent."

Recognizing Your Emotional Patterns and Tracking Your Growth

By now, you may realize that self-awareness is the core of emotional Intelligence, quietly shaping how you parent and partner. The goal is to tune into the signals your body and mind send out, especially when your day feels like a runaway train.

Notice moments when you catch yourself snapping at your child, or criticizing your partner, only to realize that you were frustrated about something else. Learn to spot subtle physical shifts, like a clenching jaw and pounding heart, that signal your emotions are about to take charge. This awareness gives you a precious few seconds to decide how you want to respond rather than reacting on autopilot.

BUILD SELF-AWARENESS OF DAILY EMOTIONS WITH PRACTICAL TOOLS AND TECHNIQUES

Developing self-awareness isn't reserved for yogis or therapists. Let's explore practical techniques that make a real difference, even for parents running on little sleep and a lot of caffeine.

Increase EQ By Journaling. Each night, jot down two things: "What made me feel proud or content?" "What left me irritated or stressed?" When you do this daily, you'll see patterns of what triggers you and what helps steady yourself. (see APA list: 2).

You may notice that mornings are always more challenging or that specific homework battles push your buttons. These insights enable you to plan by building in a quiet pause before the daily rush or by tackling tough conversations after a snack.

Raising your EQ is about being self-aware and honest with yourself, while being intentional with others. The more you practice, the more control you feel as you weather life's storms. And you teach your child, by example, how to follow your lead.

Raise Self Awareness With A Reflective Meditation. This doesn't have to mean sitting cross-legged in silence for an hour. Even a couple of minutes with your eyes closed while focusing on your breath can help you notice what's swirling inside.

Ask yourself, "What am I feeling right now?" "Where do I feel it in my body?" Sometimes, simply naming the emotion — such as anger, frustration, or disappointment — can help soften its grip.

The more often you check in like this, the more natural it feels to pause before venting angst on tender ears.

Catch Your Child Being Good As Often As Possible To Reinforce Productive Behavior. This nudges your mind away from scanning for problems and toward noticing small moments of kindness and effort. What you focus on expands. When you praise your child for sharing with a sibling or cleaning up without being asked, you also train your brain to look for positives in stressful situations. Over time, your mood shifts. You start seeing more good in your day and less of what drags you down.

Consider A Convincing Link Between Self-Awareness And Emotional Control. When you get better at noticing what triggers your anger and overwhelm, you're less likely to fall into reactive parenting. Instead of yelling when shoes are lost for the third time this week, perhaps you realize that you're worried about being late for work. A simple pause gives you a chance to breathe, consider your choices, and then respond calmly.

Personal growth starts with an awareness of old patterns. Ask yourself, "Do I raise my voice when I feel ignored?" Do I withdraw or freeze when tension builds?" "Do I automatically attribute negative meanings to things people say and do?"

Seeing patterns creates space for change. When you set personal goals for emotional growth, finding patterns helps you stay focused and celebrate progress. Suppose you decide this week to pause and count to five before responding under stress. Perhaps you ask your child how they feel before launching into advice or discipline. Each small goal fulfilled produces feel-good brain chemicals and helps you grow in confidence with momentum, day after day.

CREATE SMOOTHER INTERACTIONS WITH A COMMUNICATION CYCLE MAP

Picture this communication cycle:

One person speaks, fully aware of the effect they want their words to have on the listener.

The listener expresses the gist of what they heard before responding in turn.

This communication flow reduces misunderstandings and reminds everyone involved to pay attention and truly listen to each other.

What if things get heated? Return to the start:

Speak with your intended effect in mind. Listen. Express the gist. Respond. It's not foolproof, but it's reliably effective, even in tough talks.

PROTECT YOUR CHILD BY ADHERING VIGILANTLY TO ONE COMMUNICATION RULE:

A parent never tells their child something critical, vindictive, or negative about the other parent, even if the disclosure were accurate. Why not?

A child identifies half of their being with one parent and half with the other, perhaps because half of a child's DNA comes from each parent. It may be the human implication of the physics concept, **Quantum Entanglement**, when two or more particles become linked, the state of one instantly influences the other, regardless of distance.

Regardless of the reasons, psychologists warn that when one parent (biological or not) targets the other parent in negative disclosures that they reveal to their child, the offending parent's revelations wound that half of the child's identity. You can avoid plunging a psychological knife into half of your child's heart by adhering to this communication rule. No exceptions.

What if damaging comments have already been made? You can repair the damage and rebuild trust, using the next science-backed strategy.

HELP A CHILD RECOVER FROM HURTFUL INTERACTIONS WITH A "MAGIC RATIO"

A parent can try to undo the harm they inflicted on a child by saying a single negative insult or criticism of the child's other parent, using this proven strategy.

It takes a "magic ratio" of five positive interactions (like expressing gratitude, showing affection, interest, and support, using gentle humor, apologizing sincerely) to counteract the effects of one negative interaction (like badmouthing your co-parent, denying responsibility for your actions, using hostile humor, refusing to engage, or criticizing your child). The magic ratio stems from clinical findings based on crucial research on relationships and parenting by psychological researcher and clinician, **John Gottman.** (see APA list: 68)

To protect your child from harm, parents must refrain from taking abusive actions or making critical comments about each other in front of their child. If you can't say or do anything positive, don't say anything negative, either in words or in body language, and refrain from abusive behavior.

What if your negative words or actions already caused harm? Consider apologizing. "I'm sorry that I was critical of your (father or mother). I won't do this again." Your child will track your progress in keeping your promise. You can, too. Why is this a wise choice?

PROMOTE PROGRESS BY TRACKING PROGRESS EXERCISE

What gets measured gets improved. To measure progress, keep a simple chart or checklist, and mark days when interactions go well with your child, partner, colleague, or even a neighbor.

List and celebrate small wins, such as managing to stay calm during a sibling squabble or apologizing after an argument, instead of letting resentment fester.

Over time, minor improvements accumulate and spill over into every area of your life. Your child (and your partner) will notice that you're showing up differently, more present, more patient, and more able to handle life's curveballs with peace instead of panic.

How does the anger-management method of self-awareness produce lasting results? The more you practice self-awareness, the easier it becomes to recognize what triggers you and to take the recommended actions to restore your calm balance, using the tools, techniques, and exercises you explore in each chapter of this workbook.

EMPATHY IN PARENTING: WALK IN YOUR CHILD'S SHOES

Trying to sense what another person is feeling, even when their experience differs from yours, is empathy in action. In parenting, empathy involves tuning into a child's emotions, letting them know that their feelings are important and matter.

Advising a child how to fix problems doesn't work as well as your calm presence does. Being present shows your child that you understand where they're coming from. When you practice empathy, you build an emotional bridge that connects you and your child. This makes it easier to communicate during challenging times.

Responding with empathy to your child's tears or frustration is easier than you may think. Saying, "I can see you're upset that your tower fell over," teaches your child that their feelings are safe with you. Saying, "You can tell me anything," encourages a child to open up, confide in you, and return for more support.

Over time, empathy builds closeness that lasts far beyond childhood. It helps children feel seen and accepted, which develops genuine self-worth. Trust grows in the soil of empathy, and so does emotional connection. Children who feel understood by their parents are more likely to share their joys and worries with them. They're less likely to act out in ways that create distance.

Communicating with empathy in interactions with your co-parent or partner can enrich your relationship. Instead of power struggles and shouting matches, empathy-based communication creates space for honest exchanges of feelings and ideas, even on complex topics. When you listen for the feeling beneath a behavior, you may respond with compassion instead of criticism.

Talking consistently to each other, as if you love one another and are each other's greatest cheerleaders, teaches your child, by example, how people who love each other communicate with warmth and loving kindness.

STRENGTHEN YOUR EMPATHY MUSCLE EXERCISES

Practice "Active Listening" in Parenting To Develop Empathy. You shut off distractions, such as your phone. You look in your child's eyes and focus on what they're saying. You don't have to agree with their point of view. Just show that you're listening. Simple phrases like "That sounds hard" and "Tell me more about what happened" invite your child to open up further. Try not to jump in with advice or correction. That doesn't work like your quiet presence does. Sit with their feelings for a while before responding. Sometimes, just being heard is all a child needs to feel better. **Jot down in your Manage Anger With Love Journal how you felt and how your child responded as you practice active listening.**

Shift Your Perspective To Enhance Empathy. Imagine what it would feel like to be your child in a specific moment. Think about a time when you felt misunderstood as a child. What did you wish an adult would say or do for you? Try swapping roles for a few minutes. Let your child be the parent, and you play the part of the upset child. You may be surprised by what comes out in this playful role reversal. It's a window into how your child experiences your words, actions, and presence.

Empathetic parenting has challenges. Your child's feelings may trigger your discomfort or impatience. You may want to solve things quickly because seeing your child upset is painful, or because you're tired after a long day. You may feel like showing too much empathy is perceived as weakness and undermines your authority. The goal is to find a balance between being understanding and firmly holding boundaries.

How can you be firm and empathetic? Do both in a compound sentence. "I know it upsets you to leave the park, but it's time to go home for dinner." This response validates the feeling and maintains the necessary rule.

Learn how to support your child without absorbing their emotions as your burden. Learn to let it go. After an emotional conversation, take a quiet moment to recharge. Listen to music that lifts your mood. Get some fresh air. Take the energy you absorbed and shake it out of your body into the earth. Releasing that angst energy ensures that it doesn't bring you down when you give your child a safe place to land.

ASK A MAGICAL QUESTION TO A STRESSED CHILD

When your child comes to you for help, be sure to ask this magical question: "Do you want to be heard, helped, or hugged?" Then, respond accordingly.

Stay Calm In Chaos With Emotional Regulation Techniques

In parenting, emotional regulation may feel like holding onto your last nerve while the world tests your patience. The goal is to navigate your emotions when challenges arise, without getting stuck in negativity. Staying calm is essential, since your mood sets the tone at home.

Children mirror what they see more than what they're told. How you manage your emotions builds the foundation for how they'll handle theirs. When you stay level-headed in sibling squabbles or spilled juice, you show a child that chaos doesn't have to control the day. Being able to regulate big feelings prevents arguments from spiraling.

It helps the entire family feel safer, calmer, seen, and understood when you make it a habit to regulate emotions effectively.

REGULATE TENSE EMOTIONS WITH PRACTICAL TECHNIQUES

When tension builds, utilize a reliable technique. Pause before things escalate. Then ease your tense nerves by practicing one of these techniques:

Tap Into The Power Of Your Breath With Deep Breathing Techniques, Such As Box Breathing. Inhale for four counts. Hold for four. Exhale for four. Hold for four. Repeat 4-4-4-4 breathing for two minutes to reset your brain and body. Try caressing your heart with one hand while your other hand caresses your crown as you breathe. This aligns your heart and brain energy. It moves you beyond survival mode to find a more thoughtful response.

Tense And Relax Muscles In Progression. Tense each muscle group from your toes upward for a few seconds, then release. This process of tensing and then releasing feet, legs, hands, and shoulders brings waves of relaxation and relieves anxiety. **This exercise can be transformed into a child-friendly game.**

RECLAIM CALM IN THE PRESENT MOMENT EXERCISES

You can reclaim calm by grounding yourself in the NOW. How? Step outside, wiggle your toes as you ground your feet in the grass. Pay attention to bird songs, clouds, and the scents of flowers. While indoors, you can focus your senses on the texture of a table, the shape of a candle, and the sounds of the family. Why get your senses involved?

Ground Your Focus To Anchor Yourself in the NOW, telling your body and brain that you're safe. Sensory experiences, such as sipping cold water or taking a hot shower, can shift your focus from runaway thoughts to being present in the moment, when all is well and as it should be.

Your calm presence comforts you and ripples through the entire family. When a parent self-regulates during meltdowns and conflict, a child feels safer and more secure with their emotions. They see that feelings don't have to overwhelm them. They see how stress can be managed without screaming or losing control. Your steady presence invites a child to share their difficult moments rather than hide them. This strengthens family bonds and builds trust, day after day.

REDUCE FAMILY TENSION WITH QUICK DAILY EXERCISES

"There are only two ways to live your life. One is as though nothing is a miracle. The other is as though everything is a miracle." **Famous quotes like this one, falsely credited to Albert Einstein, are so common they're called "Neinsteins".**

Neinstein's Miracle, attributed to Anatoly Dverin (a Ukrainian-American born in 1935), inspired me to practice seeing miracles as a daily exercise that rewires the brain from a stressed, survival state to one of peaceful calm, where love thrives.

OPEN YOUR EYES TO "NEINSTEIN'S" MIRACLES: IS EVERYTHING OR NOTHING A MIRACLE IN YOUR EYES?

My views have evolved through the years. My childhood view of miracles included the resurrection of the dead, restoring sight to the blind, walking on water, and turning water into wine. As an adult, exploring **A Course In Miracles by Helen Schucman** expanded my view of practical miracles, which include replacing an unloving thought, feeling, or action with a loving one. That's a basic premise for how parents manage anger with love and guide a child to do the same.

A first step is to introduce a child (or yourself) to the idea of seeing everything as a miracle. For instance, when my children were toddlers, I often said, **"Our body is a healing miracle machine"**. And we'd express thanks when we observed how it heals a cut or a cold, develops a baby, makes us stronger, shows us stories as we sleep, solves problems, and turns the food we eat into energy we use to make it a great day. This view helped my young children feel like they are living miracles, as they truly are.

I often showed my toddlers the miracle of a perception shift during our **"Beauty Patrol,"** by pointing out beauty all around us, such as the tiny purple flowers poking through the snow, the fireball sun setting behind our trees, the hummingbird's wings beating four thousand times a minute, while hovering by a flower, or twelve thousand times a minute, while doing a courtship dive.

I helped my children see abundant miracles in what we call **"Simple Pleasures,"** such as the smell of banana bread we baked together, the feel of a cool breeze on the skin, the taste of fresh raspberries (our "earth candy"), and the warmth of holding hands. Savoring simple pleasures with all the senses deepens emotional satisfaction and a sense of safety, which nourish love. This creates a miracle shift from stress to love amidst the quiet beauty of daily life.

What happens when you practice seeing the beauty of practical miracles and savoring simple pleasures as a family? A child quickly learns to notice them and feel thankful, producing feel-good brain chemicals. This trains a child's brain to focus on more things they like each day rather than on what they don't. What they focus on grows.

What happens when a parent savors the beauty of simple pleasures and replaces unloving thoughts with loving ones? This miracle shift in perception makes it easier to stay calm during a child's tantrum and talk through their big emotions without getting lost in their stormy sea. You're teaching by example how to ride life's waves without capsizing.

What if you don't see miracles, yet you'd like to? Try the next exercise.

WELCOME MIRACLES DAILY EXERCISE

Soon after you wake up, generate enthusiasm as you say this out loud:

I'M OPEN TO RECEIVING MIRACLES TODAY.

I'M OPEN TO BEING SURPRISED BY JOY.

I'M THANKFUL FOR SEEING SIGNS SAYING, "I'M ON THE RIGHT PATH."

THANK YOU FOR MY BLESSINGS. THANK YOU FOR MY

LESSONS. THANK YOU FOR MY MIRACLES TODAY AND EVERY DAY.

During the day, look for glimmers of awe, signs of hope, chances to scatter joy, and evidence of practical miracles, including each shift from feeling anger or fear to peace and love. Opening your eyes to miracles for 60 consecutive days forms a new habit you love that loves you back through the loving eyes of your child.

MAKE A PRACTICAL SHIFT INTO CALM WITH AN ENERGETIC RELEASE

LET GO OF ANGER AND ANXIETY IN A ONE-MINUTE EXERCISE

Massage the web of your left thumb firmly, in small circles, for 30 seconds, or until the tenderness eases. Repeat this on your right thumb web. Massaging these acupressure points releases angst energy and creates a soothing sense of calmness in your body and brain. It works for your child when you teach it to them.

TEACH YOUR CHILD EMOTIONAL INTELLIGENCE, STEP BY STEP

Among the most valuable gifts you give a child is teaching Emotional Intelligence. This helps children manage emotions, connect with others, and solve problems. It builds confidence in handling friendships, school, future jobs, and even parenting. While it won't eliminate all emotional drama, children will be better prepared to rebound from setbacks and manage big feelings without being overwhelmed. How do you begin the process?

Identifying emotions together is the first step in teaching Emotional Intelligence. A child doesn't inherently know what anger, sadness, or frustration is. They need help expressing their feelings in words. If your child clenches their fists or frowns, you might mirror it and say, "You look mad right now."

Use movies, storybooks, or daily events to name emotions. Making faces in a mirror can be a game, "Guess That Feeling." As your child's vocabulary and awareness grow, so does their ability to see how emotions may either deplete or energize them.

Encouraging emotional expression is equally important. A child may be reluctant to discuss their feelings, so offer them a menu of options. Invite your child to draw a picture or listen to music that matches their mood. Dancing frustration or painting happiness can allow expression beyond words. Some children prefer writing notes, using toys, or acting out scenarios with puppets. The more creative outlets you suggest, the more natural it is to share feelings.

Modeling Emotional Intelligence Is Essential. Your actions teach more than any lecture. In conflicts, show your child how to pause, take a breath, and choose a calm response.

What if you lose your temper? Admit it. "I yelled because I was frustrated. I'll try to take a breath next time." Your honesty demonstrates that regrettable actions happen and repair is possible.

Transforming conflict into connection takes effort that yields lasting results. Instead of punishing a child for an outburst, start focusing on the feeling behind their behavior. "You're upset that screen time is over. Endings can be tough." It's essential to be clear. "Feeling angry is natural, but hitting your sister when you're angry is not acceptable." Children learn that all feelings are acceptable, but not all behaviors are.

Raising Emotionally Intelligent Children Is A Challenge. They may refuse to talk, push back, or test your patience. Every time you respond with patience and curiosity instead of anger or shame, you reinforce the truth that feelings are not inherently dangerous. You might share a simile that children like. As you gaze at the blue sky with big clouds, say, "Feelings are like clouds moving across the blue sky. You are the blue sky. Clouds of emotion pass by. Bye-bye (name an emotion)."

Teaching Emotional Intelligence Pays Off In Everyday Moments. Your child comforts a friend, apologizes for hurting someone, and shares their worries with you instead of bottling them up. A child recovers faster from tough days when they know their feelings pass by and support is available. They become better problem solvers, able to pause, consider options, and ask for help. These skills support academic success, improve social skills, and build stronger emotional bonds.

Making Room For These Practical Shifts In Your Busy Days Is Worth The Effort. Teaching emotional intelligence is about being present and learning together in the quiet moments of an active life. If you commit to practicing these techniques, which build emotional resilience in happy relationships, until they become second nature, then your child will follow your lead.

Next, you'll explore a system that helps you swap a negative-thinking habit with one that lets you respond more effectively to anger, stress, and overwhelm.

CHAPTER 3

COGNITIVE BEHAVIORAL TECHNIQUES FOR PARENTS

UNDERSTANDING CBT: A PARENT'S GUIDE

IMAGINE YOU'RE MAKING BREAKFAST, and your child spills maple syrup all over the freshly cleaned floor. Your first instinct might be to snap or scold. You can catch that reaction and redirect it with Cognitive Behavioral Therapy (CBT). It's a practical toolkit that helps you notice patterns between thoughts, feelings, and actions. At its core, CBT guides you toward more peaceful family moments. (see APA list: 9)

CBT is based on a powerful principle: Your thoughts influence how you feel, and those feelings, in turn, guide your actions. This "thoughts-emotions-behaviors" loop unfolds in milliseconds. For instance, if you interpret your child's whining as "They never respect me," you likely will feel resentment and respond harshly. If, instead, you see it as "My child feels overwhelmed," you may react calmly.

Recent science suggests that what you focus on can feed growth and influence outcomes in surprising ways, as you see at home. What you focus on grows.

CBT provides tools to pause and challenge unhelpful thoughts. It's not about ignoring reality or pretending everything is fine. Instead, it's noticing an automatic thought ("I'm a terrible parent") and trading it for a more balanced one ("This is a tough moment, but I'll get through it").

Over time, this habit of replacing an automatic, unhelpful thought with a more balanced one rewires your brain's response to stress, so that anger is not your first reaction.

CBT is a genuine game-changer for parents, especially when old habits or knee-jerk reactions surface during times of stress.

CBT techniques are designed for use in everyday life, not just during therapy sessions. You might use them during a carpool argument, a bedtime struggle, or a tense conversation with your co-parent. For example, CBT teaches you how to step back and observe the stories running through your mind before reacting automatically. This lets you respond in a way that aligns with your values, rather than your stress.

What does the science say? CBT research shows the brain is capable of change at any age through **neuroplasticity** in response to Cognitive Behavior Therapy. (see APA list: 11) Practicing CBT forms new brain pathways, making it easier to access calm thinking, even as your nervous system's alarm bells go off.

Over time, the brain shifts from an automatic fight-or-flight mode to a more problem-solving and logical-thinking mode. You don't force yourself to calm down. You train your brain to do so.

CBT also models emotional regulation for your children, as they watch and learn from your example. As they see you pause and rethink a situation, instead of exploding, they pick up those skills themselves. This contagious calm strengthens family bonds and offers more emotional breathing room.

EXPERIMENT WITH TWO KEY CBT TECHNIQUES

Cognitive Restructuring helps you examine whether your thoughts are genuine or simply old habits. You gently challenge beliefs that fuel anger, trading them for healthier ones.

Exposure Therapy helps you gradually face situations that trigger strong reactions. Your brain learns they're not so threatening so that you can remain calm.

REWIRE ANGRY THOUGHT PATTERNS EXERCISE

See how a quick reflection improves thinking habits. Think of a parenting situation this week that made you angry. What story did you tell yourself in that moment? "My child never listens." Or, "I can't handle this."

Then write down your thought, the emotion it created, and how you reacted. Was your reaction helpful? If not, what's a better alternative that you could try next time? This quick reflection helps you reprogram unhelpful thought habits.

CBT doesn't require a lot of time, yet it does require a lot of willingness to notice what's happening inside, and try out new responses. With practice, reflection becomes second nature, helping you shift from reactivity to thoughtful, productive actions.

IDENTIFY YOUR COGNITIVE DISTORTIONS THAT FUEL ANGER

Parenting often can feel like a series of frustrations, both big and small. These daily stressors make it easy to fall into **Cognitive Distortions,** which are automatic, negative thinking patterns that fuel anger and drain energy, often without you realizing it.

Before you can replace thoughts that don't serve you with those that do, it's essential to identify if you exhibit any of these Cognitive Distortions:

Overgeneralizing is a common pitfall. It takes one incident and turns it into a blanket statement about yourself or your child. For instance, after your child ignores you once, you might think, "They never listen." This thought lets one incident overshadow everything else.

Catastrophizing is another frequent distortion. It blows up a minor mishap, like spilled milk, into a big deal, convincing yourself, "This always happens. I'll never have peace." This mindset allows common issues to overwhelm you.

Complaining only magnifies problems. Habitually venting about your partner not helping or your teenager's messy room makes minor annoyances seem bigger. This consistent focus on negatives impacts your mood by producing cortisol, colors your interactions with your family, and causes your brain to seek out further evidence to support your negative beliefs.

Seeing mistakes as disasters, rather than learning opportunities, causes a downfall of happiness, power and success. This traps you in a cycle of disappointment. If your child forgets their lunch or you lose your temper, you count this as proof of a failure, instead of a chance to see and grow from its lesson.

Focusing attention on negatives determines your emotions. The more you focus on negative thoughts, the more powerful these feelings become as you reinforce negativity. You might snap at your partner, then wonder why everyone seems tense. This pattern of negative thoughts leading to intense emotions and regretful choices can leave you feeling stuck and exhausted.

BREAK DISTORTED THINKING HABITS THROUGH AWARENESS EXERCISES

Make a daily habit of writing in your **Manage Anger With Love Journal,** whether in a notebook or your phone's notes app, to help you identify patterns. Jot down your distorted thoughts without judgment. Soon, patterns emerge and show you which thought distortions most often affect you. This insight guides you to your next step.

Question Your Repeating, Painful Thoughts TECHNIQUES

Try a practical approach of Socratic questioning. Ask yourself, "Is this thought true? What evidence supports or weakens it?" Maybe you think, "My child never listens." Now pause to recall the times they have. Consider alternative explanations. Is your child tired or distracted, but not disrespectful? This pause to question opens space for empathy, insight, and understanding.

Challenge an anger-provoking thought in greater depth with a tool that amplifies Socratic questioning. Continue asking Byron Katie's four liberating questions about a worrisome thought: "Is it true? Can I absolutely know it's true? How do I react when I believe that thought? Who would I be and how would I behave without that thought?" Answering these questions in honest reflection loosens the grip of limiting thoughts. This frees you to take the next step.

Reframe Your Reactions to Parenting Stressors With Two Power Tools:

Shift your thinking with "Cognitive Restructuring". Parenting chaos might strike when your child loudly refuses to wash up for dinner. A defiant tone can trigger automatic tension, causing you to snap without questioning your thoughts. You might think, "They always try to upset me," or "I'm a fool to think they'll do as I ask." Ask yourself, "Is my thought based on a fact or a feeling?" "What's my evidence to support it?" "What example contradicts the evidence?" After you challenge the truth in an automatic thought by questioning it, you may shift how you think, feel, and respond by taking the next step.

Consider different responses with "Perspective-taking." It may feel odd at first. You pause, breathe, and try to see the situation from your child's point of view. Or imagine how you'll look back at this moment in the future. Consider what else might be true. Did your child have a tough day? Is something else on their mind? This doesn't excuse bad behavior. It provides a more accurate response that lowers emotional intensity.

DEVELOP A PERSPECTIVE-TAKING HABIT EXERCISE

1. Notice what triggers you by identifying the automatic thought.
2. Ask yourself whether that thought is accurate or just a knee-jerk reaction.
3. Try out a more neutral or constructive explanation.

4. Respond based on this revised perspective.

For instance, you see a messy room and think, "He's lazy." Then pause to reconsider. "He might feel overwhelmed with everything right now. Maybe we can tackle this together." You may notice an immediate difference in how this perspective affects your words, tone, body language, and action plan.

When you model flexible thinking, your child learns that situations aren't black and white. They see that you don't have to act on every emotion. A child may follow your lead after seeing how your choices create harmony at home.

Consider The Benefits And Misconceptions Of Reframing

Reframing how you view an incident doesn't mean you ignore emotions or thoughts. You discover a new interpretation that helps reduce anger and stress. Deciding to see a child's stubbornness as determination, or their tall tales as creativity, enables you to stay calmer and respond constructively. Reframing creates opportunities for emotional connection and promotes personal growth in you and your child.

What the brain science says: Brain scans show that reframing emotions and thoughts activates the part of your brain that keeps your emotions calm and your thinking clear. Suppressing emotions, in contrast, activates the stress circuits. This one shift in how you process emotion can reduce your long-term stress load. So brain science provides an incentive to build the habit of reframing. (see APA list: 50)

Each time you practice reframing, you get better at handling difficult parenting moments with calm and confidence. Your reactions become more about who you want to be as a parent, not just old habits. Over time, tense moments lose their grip, and your family life shifts in lasting, positive ways.

PRACTICE NEW RESPONSES WITH BEHAVIORAL ACTIVATION EXERCISES

When you feel anger rising, it's easy to get stuck in a loop of old habits, like snapping, yelling, withdrawing, rolling eyes, or muttering under your breath. Fortunately, you can train yourself out of these patterns. How?

Practicing Behavioral Activation is all about acting differently, even when your mind is swirling with frustration. When you change what you do, you can change what you feel. The more you try new behaviors, the easier it gets to break free from the grip of an automatic anger reaction.

Behavioral activation is intentionally choosing constructive actions, especially when your emotions could drag you down. If you retreat when things get heated, consider walking closer and calmly stating your needs. If your habit is to criticize, try being curious by asking a question instead. You listen until your child has finished answering. Then you respond.

Over time, new responses feel more comfortable. Your brain rewires itself with every new effort, making positive behavior more of a reflex and less of a struggle.

TRY ROLE-PLAYING TO BUILD NEW RESPONSES EXERCISE

You can start by thinking of a common scenario that triggers your reaction. Perhaps your child interrupts you while you're on the phone, or refuses to get ready for bed. Rather than waiting until the next blow-up, you rehearse how you'd like to respond to that scenario. You can do this alone in a mirror or with a partner who pretends to be your child. Say out loud what you wish you'd said last time. "I see you're excited, but I need two more minutes." This says you're aware of their feelings yet you also honor yours.

This rehearsal prepares your brain for real-life moments, so when chaos strikes again, you're ready with words and tone that match your best intentions. If you have older children or a partner willing to play along, you swap roles and see the situation from their viewpoint, building empathy and flexibility.

SOLVE A PROBLEM EXERCISES

This is a game-changing strategy for parents. Instead of focusing on the problem itself, like constant backtalk or sibling spats, focus on concrete solutions.

Sit down when things are calm and brainstorm options together. "What can we do differently tomorrow morning to avoid the rush?" Involve your children, if they're old enough. Children love contributing ideas and often may surprise you with creative fixes.

Write down three possible solutions for each recurring issue, no matter how silly they seem at first. Your pre-teen suggests setting the breakfast table the night before. Your partner offers to prepare lunch while you look for a missing shoe. Testing new ideas as a family builds teamwork and fosters a sense of everyone having a role in maintaining harmony.

Use repetition as a key to success. New behaviors may feel clumsy, like trying to write with your non-dominant hand. It takes practice to make it permanent. Rehearse strategies during neutral times, not when arguments arise. Try calm statements. "Let's try that again, using kind words." "I need a minute before we talk about this."

Choose a pre-planned exit strategy to use when you find yourself about to lose your cool. Step outside or splash water on your face. Little rituals can remind you to pause and reset. Your child sees the effects.

Consider writing out scripts to anchor new habits. Jot down phrases that reflect the parent you want to be. "I know this is hard for both of us. Let's figure this out together." "I'm frustrated, yet I won't yell." Keep these reminders on your fridge or phone until they become natural responses.

Practice alternative responses to enhance your social skills. When your child sees you handle anger with composure and creativity, they learn self-regulation and problem-solving by example.

RELEASE A TRIGGER EXERCISE

Pick one recurring trigger from your week, such as bedtime battles, after-school meltdowns, or a daily irritant. For the next three days, commit to trying one new response each time that trigger arises. Reflect each evening. How did I do? How did everyone react? What could I do better tomorrow? When I took that new action, how did it change the results? Make mental notes or actual notes in your journal.

With practice, behavioral activation becomes more like muscle memory with less effort. Each small win, such as one less shout or one more calm conversation, strengthens your belief that positive change is happening. And every effort counts as a step forward.

TRACK PROGRESS WITH TOOLS FOR MONITORING CHANGE

Teaching children new skills reveals how progress comes in small steps. Parenting growth is similar. Self-monitoring your positive changes promotes more. When you track your growth, each positive step is reinforced, making new habits stick as you let old patterns fade away. Paying attention to these changes keeps you motivated, especially when you give yourself credit for choosing calm and responding better in each challenging situation.

Experiment with various methods to monitor emotional and behavioral shifts until you find what works best for your life.

Technology makes self-monitoring easier than ever. There are emotion-tracking apps that log moods, triggers, and reactions in seconds. With a quick tap, you can note whether you stayed patient during the morning rush or lost your cool at night. Over time, these tracking records reveal patterns. Monday can be a challenge to your patience, or certain routines may be particularly stressful. The statistics may help guide you in adjusting your routines, expectations, and self-care strategies. (see APA List: 47)

Journaling each week adds an extra layer to what digital tools may overlook. Devote several minutes each week to jot down what went well, what was difficult, and what you learned about yourself. To boost confidence on tough days, re-read journal entries about victories and lessons learned. Re-read your answers to Byron Katie's four questions that challenge limiting thoughts and beliefs.

Wearing tracking technology is another practical tool for busy parents. Ring.Conn tracks sleep states, stress, heart rate, brain oxygen levels, and daily steps, all without requiring a subscription fee.

Monitoring your sleep scores shows you when tiredness fuels frustration and a short temper. You can track how making even minor tweaks, such as going to bed earlier or taking a midday nap, can have a positive impact on your patience and mood. Look for patterns and progress, noting examples in your journal.

Seeking partner feedback is invaluable. Instead of guessing where you stand, will you ask for direct input? Regular feedback sessions with your partner, perhaps during a quiet Sunday, offer opportunities to share what's working and where things feel stuck. Keep discussions positive and solution-oriented to avoid blame and build understanding. Keep doing what works. Stop doing what doesn't.

Seeking feedback from children is just as significant. Schedule casual check-ins to discuss what's going well at home. Notice when your child does something positive, such as sharing, using kind words, or helping without being asked. Offer specific praise. "I saw you calm yourself when your brother took your game. That took real patience." This honest encouragement not only boosts their self-esteem but also motivates them to repeat the same behavior.

Celebrating everyday wins fuels long-term motivation. You don't have to throw a party every time you avoid yelling. Mini acknowledgments, like a favorite snack, a high-five, or a relaxed family movie night, help keep spirits up and motivation strong.

For bigger milestones, such as a month without shouting during homework, create a reward everyone can look forward to, like a special excursion or letting your child choose dinner. Celebrate progress with genuine joy, so the entire family feels encouraged to move forward and learn from joyful experiences that arise more often than painful ones did in the past. Remember, what you focus on grows. (see APA list: 37)

REFLECT ON PROGRESS EXERCISE

One time each week, spend five minutes alone or with your partner to reflect:

- What did I handle better this week?
- When did I catch myself before reacting?
- Which new skill feels the most natural?
- What patterns did I notice in my mood or stress levels?
- What small thing can I celebrate this week?
- What might become a new habit that I love?

Even one note of progress proves change is taking place, gradually but surely.

Let's recap: Your goal is to observe growth and adopt positive changes as you go. When you repeat a new action every day for two months, you establish a habit you love and that loves you back, enriching your interactions and shifting family dynamics.

Next, you'll discover how to adjust anger management strategies as you face toddler tantrums, pre-teen limit tests, and teenage attitudes.

CHAPTER 4
AGE-SPECIFIC STRATEGIES TO MANAGE ANGER

TANTRUMS AND TODDLERS: ANGER MANAGEMENT WITH LITTLE ONES

PICTURE THIS: You're in the checkout line, with a crowd behind you. Suddenly, your toddler starts screaming, red-faced. You feel every eye on you. Your pulse races. You wonder how such a small person can unleash such big feelings.

Do you know how vulnerable and embarrassed you can feel in this moment? You're not alone. Even the most patient among us is tested by toddler tantrums. They aren't a sign of "bad behavior" or poor parenting. Tantrums are a natural stage in child development, rooted in biology and brain growth. When you understand the why behind your child's outburst, you can shift your frustration to compassion. Then respond with more calm and confidence.

Toddlers live in a world where their emotions are enormous, but their ability to control them is minuscule. Imagine having a desire you can't express, being hungry or tired but unable to say so, or seeing your toy snatched away but not knowing how to get it back. That's life for a toddler, whose brain is under construction, especially the parts responsible for self-regulation and impulse control.

Most little ones can't put their feelings into words yet, so when frustration, disappointment, or confusion arise, it all comes out in one dramatic show. Their attention spans are fleeting. A minor setback feels overwhelming because they haven't learned to pause or cope with it. The inability to articulate their needs, whether it's hunger, boredom, or wanting a blue cup instead of a green one, often results in intense feelings erupting as screams.

EXPLORE TOOLS TO MANAGE TODDLER ANGER

Being proactive can reduce the likelihood of a tantrum. Children thrive on predictability. When you have steady routines for meals, naps, playtime, bathtime, and bedtime, toddlers know what to expect and feel more secure. This structure builds their trust and lowers the tension that triggers outbursts.

Offering choices is another powerful tool. Instead of barking orders, you empower your child to make small decisions. "Do you want the red shirt or the yellow one?" "Should we brush your teeth before or after your bath?" Making choices gives toddlers a sense of control and autonomy. They are less likely to resist when they feel their voice matters.

Even with preparation, tantrums will happen. When they do, your response shapes how quickly and peacefully the storm passes. The most effective tool you have is your own calm. Speaking in a soft voice can soothe frazzled nerves, including yours.

Try kneeling to your child's level so you're eye-to-eye and say something like, "I see you're upset. You wanted the blue cup." This simple acknowledgment helps your toddler feel understood, which often eases their distress.

Shifting focus also helps. "Let's find your teddy together." "Will you help me stack these books?" Distracting focus works wonders for young children, whose attention tends to bounce from one thing to another.

What if your toddler is too upset to listen? Stay nearby. Let them know you're there when they're ready—no lecturing at the peak of a tantrum. A toddler's brain can't process logic, while emotions flood their system. Instead, maintain a steady tone and wait for the storm to settle naturally. (see APA list: 13)

How you handle your feelings during these meltdowns teaches your child more than words ever could. Show your child how to breathe deeply through their nose. Breathe in through the nose for four counts. Exhale through the nose for four counts. Invite your toddler to join you in doing this. Sometimes, a gentle touch helps restore calm by placing a hand on their back or holding them, if they're receptive.

CALM TODDLERS BEFORE SLEEP EXERCISE

My toddlers loved this relaxation exercise before bedtime.

Gently feather your fingertips over each area to relax as you say, "Rest your eyes… rest your ears… rest your nose… rest your elbows…" Softly say each phrase twice, guiding your child to rest their body from head to toes until tension melts away. This soothes them, nurturing a sense of safety and comfort in your presence.

DISCOVER THE POWER OF SLEEP TO REGULATE TODDLER EMOTIONS

Exhaustion makes little ones more prone to meltdowns, just as it does in adults running on empty. **Dr. Marc Weissbluth's study-backed strategies in his book, Healthy Sleep Habits, Happy Child,** stress the importance of regular nap and bedtime routines that support healthy brain development and emotional stability (APA list: 12).

Dr. Weissbluth was my children's pediatrician. He insisted we follow his sleep guidelines. I saw a dramatic impact on my children's moods and resilience when sleep was protected. "Never wake a sleeping baby" is Dr. W's mantra. Building your day around their natural rhythms works best.

BUFFER AGAINST FREQUENT TANTRUMS WITH THE BEST LOVE LANGUAGE

You may buffer the stress that triggers tantrums by identifying and speaking your child's unique "Love Language" among **The 5 Love Languages of Children.** First, you figure out what helps your toddler feel loved. Maybe it's cuddle time, kind words, helping with tasks, serving their favorite meal, or rocking them to sleep. After you uncover what lights up your toddler, then you fill their "love tank" with it every day —not only after an outburst, but also as part of everyday life. (see APA list: 54).

When a child feels securely connected and cherished in ways that make sense to them, they develop stronger emotional regulation skills and trust that you are their safe place.

REFLECT ON TANTRUMS EXERCISE

Try this exercise for one week. After your toddler has a meltdown, jot down what happened just before (missed nap? hunger? sudden change?), what strategies you tried (offering choices? deep breathing? distraction?), and how each of you felt afterward. You'll see patterns emerge, such as tantrums spiking before lunch or after playdates. Note the techniques that calmed your child.

Supporting toddlers through tantrums is about helping them manage big feelings as they grow, rather than stopping outbursts. Your calm presence and consistent loving kindness lay the groundwork for emotional resilience that serves them long after toddler tantrums have passed.

NAVIGATE ADOLESCENCE WITH PRE-TEEN ANGER MANAGEMENT STRATEGIES

Some days with pre-teens may feel like living with a different person every hour. One minute, your child talks to you about their favorite YouTuber. Next, they snap at you for asking about homework. These emotional swings aren't personal. They're part of a bigger transformation, as their brains and bodies gear up for the teenage years. Hormones surge, triggering volatile moods and a hunger for independence. Children this age crave space and autonomy, yet they still need a steady connection with you, even if they act like they don't.

Their new desire to call the shots can spark unexpected power struggles. You may notice more arguments about chores, or what's "not fair." You may sense that what their friends think now matters more than what you do. Social media tends to reinforce this. Your goal is to continue being a steady, loving presence in their life.

Setting boundaries for pre-teens doesn't mean building walls. Think of it as putting up gentle guardrails they can lean on when they wobble. Rules matter. How you deliver them guides outcomes. Be clear about expectations, such as when screens go off, how much homework needs to be completed before play, and which chores are non-negotiable as part of being a family team member. Let them know the consequences of breaking the rules, and stick to these limits without drama. At the same time, give them room to make choices within those boundaries. Negotiating privileges with them helps preteens develop a sense of responsibility.

Avoid saying, "Because I said so." Try, "If you want to stay up late on Fridays, let's talk about what needs to happen during the week." Invite their input on responsibilities. Will they help decide the family's dinner menu, or choose when to do chores? When pre-teens help set the rules, they're more likely to respect them.

Accepting that conflict with pre-teens is inevitable helps you handle it. You don't need to win every dispute. Your goal is to guide, not dominate.

Inviting conversations instead of interrogating is the most effective tool in your toolkit. How do you invite an open dialogue? Say something like, "I noticed you were upset when I asked about homework. What's going on?" Listen more than you talk. Nod, make eye contact, and let them finish speaking without interrupting.

The habit of active listening builds trust. It shows that their feelings count. Sometimes, you can defuse tension just by reflecting the gist of what you heard. "So your friend laughed at your answer in class. How did you feel about that?" This helps your child feel heard and seen, contrary to the outdated adage "Children should be seen and not heard."

Pre-teens test limits, not because they want to defy you, but because they want to explore their independence. They're figuring out who they are and where they fit in the world.

When faced with a disagreement, your challenge is to avoid taking it personally and to resist escalating it with threats or lectures. Remind yourself that anger in pre-teen years is often a mask for worry or sadness about changes happening inside and out. You can share your feelings without blame by using "I" statements. "I feel frustrated when chores aren't done, because we all have to pitch in." This invites problem-solving, without triggering defensiveness. If things get heated, consider taking a "time away" to cool off before discussing things further.

Fostering emotional expression at this age pays off long after the dust settles on a disagreement. Pre-teens need a safe space where feelings like anger, disappointment, and envy are okay to talk about. If your child is shutting down or lashing out, encourage words over outbursts. "It's alright to be mad. Let's figure out what's underneath it." (see APA list: 14)

Getting curious instead of furious means asking questions that open doors, rather than closing them with an angry outburst or harsh discipline. Ask, "What would help you feel better right now?" "Is there something at school that made today harder?" Your curiosity shifts the energy between you, turning a conflict into a search for understanding.

Knowing how peer pressure adds another layer of complexity in the pre-teen years is essential. You may find your child parroting friends' slang or mimicking group attitudes that clash with your family's values. Instead of launching into lectures about right and wrong, ask questions that prompt them to think. "What do you think made your friend act that way?" "How did it feel when you went along with the group?" This sparks reflection, helping your child build a behavior compass.

Their urge for independence can be bittersweet for parents, who still see glimpses of their cuddly little child beneath the bravado. Letting go doesn't mean letting up on connection. Schedule regular one-on-one time, even if it's just a quick walk or sharing a snack in the kitchen. This shows your pre-teen that your love doesn't depend on perfect behavior or shared interests. They may roll their eyes or act unimpressed. Yet deep down, your one-on-one moments build the bridge that lets them come back to you in any storm.

Noticing how pre-teens walk a tightrope between childhood and adolescence, sometimes teetering back and forth within the hour, promotes understanding. Your steady presence and ability to listen without judgment give them the courage to keep talking. You give them tools to handle big emotions, without shutting down or blowing up. When anger bubbles up, remember that each conflict can bring out the best in you.

EXPLORE STRATEGIES FOR HEALTHY CONFLICT IN THE TEENAGE YEARS

Teenagers can sometimes feel like strangers in their own homes, even to themselves. They're facing academic demands and social media pressures that you couldn't imagine when you were in high school. They're unraveling the mysteries of who they're becoming as their bodies and hormones change, and what kind of future they can expect amid the reported threats to the American dream and even to life as we know it on Mother Earth.

Add that stress to the pressure of your expectations, their own, their teachers', and their college's. Can you see why your curfew discussion might trigger an outburst of anger, withdrawal, or even apathy?

Social stress is another storm. Friendships shift overnight. Reputations change with a single post or rumor. Even the most confident teens can get tangled up in self-doubt when they feel they don't measure up. As parents, we may see only the surface: The eye rolls, the monosyllabic answers, the missed assignments. Below the surface lies a young person who desperately wants to be seen, heard, and accepted for who they are.

Managing conflict with teenagers is like walking a tightrope between providing structure and letting go. Consistent boundaries matter more than ever. Yet, how you enforce them needs to evolve. Will you set firm but flexible limits when possible? For instance, you might have a non-negotiable on safety (no texting while driving). Yet, you allow negotiation on less critical issues (such as later curfews on weekends, provided responsibilities are met). Instead of laying down the law unilaterally, invite your teen into problem-solving chats. Sit together. Ask for their input. "What do you think is fair?" "How would you handle consequences if you were me and our roles were reversed?" When you resist shutting down a conflict, your teen trusts that they can tell you anything.

Handling endless complaints about school rules, chores, siblings, or how "unfair" life feels is another parenting challenge. It's tempting to dismiss complaints as drama. Yet allowing endless venting, without any expectation of solutions, doesn't serve anyone. Instead, you set gentle limits that inspire new action. "I hear you're upset. Will you tell me three things that would make this better?" This encourages your teen to shift from complaining to brainstorming improvements as if it's a team effort.

Utilizing the secret weapon of empathy is wise with teens. Why? It's easy to forget what it felt like to be fifteen and you're staring down unfinished chores or missed curfews. Try to step into their shoes before reacting. Listen for what's beneath the attitude. Is it fear of failing? Is it loneliness after a falling out with friends? Validate their feelings, even if you disagree with their conclusions. "I can see why you'd be frustrated." "It sounds like you felt left out today." Accepting their feelings and views without necessarily agreeing with them allows you to acknowledge your teen's reality without lecturing or punishing them.

Flipping the script is practical and fun to try. Ask your teen to imagine how they'd feel if they were you. Invite them to share how they think you feel when they come home late without a call, or when they ignore family rules. You're not guilt-tripping. You're building understanding both ways. This can soften defensiveness and remind everyone that respecting feelings is a two-way street.

Enduring many conflicts with teens presents a test of love. How do you rebuild or maintain trust after conflict? This is where many families get stuck in silent stand-offs or cold wars that last for days. Instead of letting wounds fester, schedule regular family check-ins, such as a weekly pizza night or a Sunday breakfast, where everyone can share concerns in a safe and supportive environment. These meetings are low-pressure. Humor helps more than heavy-handed lectures. What if you overreact harshly? Apologize and say, "You didn't deserve that."

Owning your missteps, not just asking for apologies from your teen, is helpful for them to witness. When you say you'll do better ("I promise to listen before jumping in to fix it next time"), make your promises visible and measurable. **What gets measured gets improved and builds trust, day after day.**

Identifying your teen's Love Languages and "speaking" them is especially important now. Teenagers are often perceived as uninterested in hugs, kind words, family time, or favorite treats. Yet research shows that teens still crave connection, which is enhanced when we speak their love languages. (APA list: 16)

IDENTIFY YOUR TEEN'S LOVE LANGUAGE EXERCISE

Do they light up at words of affirmation? (I'm proud of how you handled that situation) Quality time? (A coffee run together) Acts of service? (Helping with a project) Physical touch? (A pat on the back) Small gifts? (Their favorite snack tucked in their bag).

Be sure to speak their love language often, even in tense moments. Encourage them to do the same for you, so you each feel loved and lovable in your relationship.

Restoring trust after conflicts requires patience and follow-through more than grand gestures. When your teen sees you're willing to keep showing up with apologies, humor, and honest effort, they learn that mistakes aren't fatal. Love doesn't disappear when things get hard. Regular check-ins, small acts of kindness in each other's language, and keeping promises (even small ones) rebuild your bridge each time conflict knocks it down. Repeating this process teaches teenagers how to repair and enrich relationships. This is a skill they'll carry with them, long after they're happily launched into adulting.

BUILD A SAFETY NET AGAINST THREATS OF HARSH CRITICISM EXERCISES

What if a history of trauma or harsh criticism auto-triggers anger in your child? A smart strategy is to seek structured support from a therapist who builds safety from threats in the body, replacing a learned threat alert with the calming effect of self-reassurance. You can support this process by guiding your child through these self-soothing exercises.

SWITCH FROM SELF-CRITICISM TO SELF-REASSURANCE EXERCISE

When your child, who has a history of harsh criticism, begins criticizing themselves over a mistake they made, you can give them tender, warm guidance in a way their brain will accept, rather than resist. You can tell your child that the frequent criticism they experienced taught their brain that mistakes were not safe, creating a habit of self-criticism. Then share the good news that old habits like self-criticism can be replaced with better ones as they practice this technique:

Whenever a child's inner critic starts acting up, suggest they say to themself, **"I'm safe. Mistakes are normal. I can learn from them."**

What does the science say? Brain scans show that this strategy lowers a child's threat and pain responses. You're helping your child believe the truth in this affirmation, which is healthy self-talk grounded in reality.

Make sure your child receives safe support from close family or friends who will give them gentle feedback. Supportive interactions help buffer their brain's vigilance against threats and, over time, reduce reactivity to criticism. So does practicing self-compassion with the next exercise.

REDUCE VIGILANCE AGAINST THE THREAT OF CRITICISM EXERCISE

Guide your child through a mini practice of self-compassion each day for a couple of months, until they form a feel-good habit of doing this solo.

Ask your child to hold their open hand against their heart. Suggest they soften their tense shoulders, and then breathe in through their nose all the love that's present. Hold the breath, feeling their heart beating with love. Ask them to breathe out their stress with a loud sigh. Finally, ask them to say three sentences. **"This is hard. I'm not alone. I can be kind to myself while I learn."**

What does the science say? Doing this mini practice regularly matters more than doing long sessions now and then. Remember, practice makes permanent for children and adults.

ADAPT YOUR COMMUNICATION STRATEGIES AS A CHILD AGES

A child's needs for connection and understanding shift as they grow, shaping how a parent must approach each conversation. What works with a toddler won't land the same way with a teenager. What feels like a breakthrough with a preschooler may fall flat with a pre-teen. Recognizing these changing communication styles is like learning new dialects as your child matures.

Toddlers process the world in pictures, sounds, and immediate feelings. They need simple words, precise gestures, and lots of repetition to grasp what's being said. A picture chart showing shoes, a coat, and a backpack can help a little one get ready much better than a long list of instructions. Pointing, demonstrating, and using hands-on cues are your best tools at this stage. When you pause to get on their level, look them in the eye, and use short sentences —like "Shoes on! Outside time!" — you build clarity about what you expect.

Teens crave authentic dialogue and a sense that you value their opinions. They're quick to spot insincerity or lectures disguised as questions. So your challenge is to ask open-ended questions that invite them to think. "What surprised you today?" "If you could change one thing about your week, what would it be?" These prompts encourage reflection, not just facts. You might not get a long answer, yet you keep the door open for next time.

Transform even the most difficult conversations into moments of genuine connection through active listening. It's easy to drift or half-listen when your mind is on duties and due dates. Yet making eye contact, leaning in, and showing genuine curiosity sends the message that your child's thoughts and feelings matter.

GET A CHILD TALKING ON DEEPER LEVELS WITH ONE HOLISTIC QUESTION:

"How are your PIES?" That's an acronym for how they feel Physically, Intellectually, Emotionally, and Spiritually.

The PIES question takes the pulse of a child's whole self, not just their grades or mood. You might ask at bedtime, "How are your PIES tonight?" Sometimes you'll get shrugs. At other times, you'll hear surprising insights about worries, hopes, things they're proud of, and things they learned. You may know what helps your child feel loved and act with kindness, which answers the Spiritual aspect of their PIES. This routine encourages in-depth discussions about the ups and downs of daily life.

Build the backbone of consistent communication through your loving presence and support. A child needs to know that no matter what happened yesterday (an argument or a request denied for their good), there will be another chance to connect today.

Regular one-on-one time with each child roars, "You matter to me." It doesn't have to be elaborate. A walk around the block or five minutes sitting on the couch goes further than you think. These moments may be opportunities to solve problems, share jokes and dreams, and even enjoy a comfortable silence together.

Make gratitude an integral part of your family's daily rhythm to deepen bonds. Expressing gratitude can create an instant emotional shift, by producing feel-good brain chemicals.

Filling a gratitude jar together, with notes about good things or kind acts, creates tangible proof of positivity in your home. Even little ones can dictate words for you to write down. "I liked playing blocks with Daddy." "Mom made my favorite pancakes." At the end of the year, or whenever spirits need lifting, you can pluck out these slips to read aloud, reminding everyone of shared wins and sweet joys. It gently shifts focus from what's lacking or going wrong to what's working and worth celebrating. What you focus on expands.

Cultivate Purpose And Reduce Teenage Anxiety With Happiness Hacks

In October 2025, Cornell disclosed findings from its six-year study of teens who were anxious and addicted to phones. The Cornell study, along with research findings from the Well-Being Lab at George Mason University, recommends this strategy. **Cultivate happiness by shifting focus from problematic inner symptoms to an outer focus on effort and progress toward purposeful pursuits.**

These science-backed findings confirm what philosophers knew. Aristotle said that the good life requires living with purpose. Nietzsche wrote, "He who has a why to live can bear almost any how." And 20th-century psychiatrist Viktor Frankl believed that his sense of purpose helped him survive Nazi concentration camps. (see APA list: 91)

How do parents help their teenager find a vital sense of purpose?

CULTIVATE PURPOSE AND REDUCE TEENAGE ANXIETY WITH A HAPPINESS HACK EXERCISE

Parents invite their teen to consider a contribution they want to make, and then help them make it, whether to the family, the community, or even themselves.

This doesn't replace mental health interventions for chronic issues. It does reveal a sure path to happiness for many teens and parents:

Stop trying to be happy and start figuring out how to make others happy. How? Brainstorm ideas with your teens. Then help them take action on their favorite ones, as you do on yours.

Will you take a moment to reflect on how the exercises you explore here make others happy, while helping you manage anger with love? This practice promotes happiness and satisfaction in all aspects of your life.

As we conclude this chapter on age-specific approaches to managing anger and communicating effectively, remember that your efforts, even on the most challenging days, build deeper bonds day after day.

What are some science-backed strategies that replace anger, stress, and overwhelm with joy, peace, and love? You'll find out in the next chapter.

CHAPTER 5
HOLISTIC APPROACHES AND QUANTUM TOOLS TO MANAGE ANGER, STRESS, AND OVERWHELM

ALBERT EINSTEIN AND NIKOLA TESLA, whose lifetimes overlapped between 1879 and 1943, each predicted that future medicine would be based on frequencies. Given what is known about energy, vibration, and frequency, let's explore holistic tools and techniques to replace lower vibrational frequencies associated with anger, fear, and overwhelm with higher vibrational frequencies associated with love, gratitude, and joy. The highest vibration always wins. It's not mystical. It's a combination of brain science, body wisdom, and quantum physics, founded by Albert Einstein, Max Planck, and Niels Bohr.

There is a metaphorical parallel between the unpredictable, rapidly changing nature of quantum energy and the sudden, unpredictable nature of emotional responses such as anger. Is it possible to harness this energy to work for you, rather than against you? Yes, by utilizing the cutting-edge tools and techniques that you will explore now.

EMOTIONAL FREEDOM TECHNIQUES: TAPPING INTO CALM

On days when emotions overwhelm you and a deep breath won't stop an angry outburst, you may get help from the Emotional Freedom Technique (EFT). Also known as "tapping", EFT involves tapping precise acupressure points on your face, hands, and upper body at the same time that you voice the issues on your mind.

This somatic (body-based) technique uses gentle tapping to send calming signals to the brain, helping release stuck emotions such as anger.

You don't need meditation experience to use EFT. Studies show that EFT lowers stress hormones, such as cortisol, lifts mood, and improves sleep and focus. In one study, those who practiced EFT experienced greater drops in anxiety and tension than those who only talked through their troubles. Today, schools and therapists use EFT to manage anger and anxiety in children and adults.

In EFT, you start by acknowledging your stress. "I'm furious my child won't listen". Or, "I feel overwhelmed by work". Then you tap each point (side of hand, eyebrow, side of eye, under eye, under nose, chin, collarbone, underarm, top of head), as you repeat a setup phrase like, "Even though I feel this anger, I accept myself."

After two rounds, end with an affirmation. "I'm open to feeling calmer now." The entire process takes a few minutes. It can be done before a meeting, after an argument, or in the car while waiting for after-school pickup.

Many parents report that EFT helps them regain composure. One mother tapped before a presentation and emerged feeling steady. Teens use it before tests and athletic endeavors. Adults may find that five minutes of tapping reduces tension and helps them respond more patiently to their children.

Guided EFT support is available for parents and teens. (see TappingSolutionFoundation.org. Founder Nick Ortner invites you to claim a 5-day gift pass to a tapping course in our Book Bonuses.

TRY A TAPPING INTO CALM EXERCISE

Identify a current stressor. Score its intensity on a scale of 1 to 10. Then tap through the points (side of hand, eyebrow, side of eye, under eye, under nose, chin, collarbone, underarm, top of head) continuously saying, "Even though I feel anger about [your situation], I accept these feelings." After two rounds, your final tapping round is an affirmation. "I'm open to feeling calmer now." Reassess your intensity. Note any changes you feel.

REPLACE OVERWHELM WITH SERENITY NOW, USING A QUANTUM TECHNIQUE

In a world built for overwhelm, finding calm can feel almost defiant. Quantum grounding acts as a reset amidst family chaos, anchoring body and mind in the present moment.

A powerful grounding method is to walk barefoot in the grass. If that's not possible, consider placing both palms on a tree or, if indoors, standing on a grounding mat, wiggling your toes, then standing on tiptoes before grounding yourself on the mat. Why?

Science suggests that our bodies respond to **Schumann Waves** —the natural frequencies of the earth and trees —which can soothe our nerves and ground us in a calm, "rest and digest" state.

When you touch a tree, its grounding energy instantly enters trillions of cells in your body. When you or your child feels stressed or anxious, a few minutes of direct contact with the earth's energy may help shift your body's energy quickly. **This isn't magic. Science says this produces measurable shifts in our stress hormones and inflammation levels.**

RESET GOALS TO PULL YOU OUT OF OVERWHELM AND BUILD MOMENTUM

Don't focus on the whole mountain. Set a Mini Goal that moves you forward to a bigger goal. Choose a single small step, such as writing two slides with bullet points for a presentation, instead of tackling the entire slide deck. Consider organizing two drawers of your child's clothes instead of tackling the whole closet. Select your mini goal. Write a clear, small step on your daily calendar. Schedule it within 24 hours as your call to action. What's the success formula?

One explicit instruction, along with 24-hour implementation, builds momentum to achieve a new mini-goal each day. Celebrating even a mini-win produces feel-good brain chemicals. How will you celebrate a mini win?

Ask yourself, "What's the most loving thing I can do for myself right now?" Do something you love that loves you back. It may be as simple as listening to a favorite podcast instead of scrolling through bad news or playing another round of video games. It may mean eating a fresh snack instead of a processed one, or choosing music and movement over more screen time.

Setting mini-goals and savoring mini-wins help serenity grow and bloom.

REDUCE ANGER AND STRESS WITH POSITIVE DISCIPLINE TECHNIQUES

Focusing on teaching rather than punishment is the foundation of positive discipline. What if your child doesn't clean up after the dog? Instead of scolding, you help them with "pup poop patrol." This approach doesn't ignore misbehavior. It allows a child to learn to do chores in a supportive way without letting anger harm their relationship with their parents. You can also redirect a child's energy and focus by suggesting an alternative activity or kindly restating expectations. Say, "Let's use our inside voices," instead of "Stop yelling." These subtle shifts create good vibrations between you.

Praising positive behavior is a strong motivator. When you notice your child making an effort or being kind, please take a moment to acknowledge it. "I see how you helped your brother. That was kind." Recognizing these moments helps build your child's self-esteem and sense of belonging. You can tie actions to outcomes by explaining logical consequences. "If you bring mud inside, we will clean it up." This isn't punishment. It's a way to teach responsibility with cause and effect.

Developing trust, patience, routine, and positive discipline without resorting to threats or fear tactics deepens parent-child bonds. Positive discipline nurtures understanding. Consistency helps your child trust and respect what you say. Family meetings to discuss rules and consequences can foster emotional growth and spark positive energy at home. This approach reduces stress, minimizes power struggles, and promotes more peaceful, emotionally-connected family time.

BREAK THROUGH SUBCONSCIOUS BLOCKS WITH THE LIFELINE TECHNIQUE: POWERED BY INFINITE LOVE AND GRATITUDE

What if stress feels stuck in your body, and anger keeps resurfacing, no matter how much you talk it out? **The Lifeline Technique by Dr. Darren Weissman** may be helpful.

This self-healing method works beneath the surface, helping you gently release emotional patterns and limiting beliefs that are buried in your subconscious, often from childhood. Instead of just "thinking positively," it asks you to notice the real feelings that are coming up.

Fear, guilt, and anger are managed with two powerful tools: Infinite Love and Gratitude. The process uses a blend of body awareness, intention-setting, and symbolic gestures (such as hand mudras or specific words) to help reconnect your mind and body. You may be surprised by how quickly old emotional wounds shift when faced with acceptance, rather than judgment.

Here's how it plays out for parents. Imagine you keep reacting harshly when your child ignores you, even though you swore you'd be calmer. The Lifeline Technique helps you trace this reaction back to times in your childhood when not being heard felt hurtful or unsafe. With practice, you learn to respond differently, rewiring your inner script.

I had a positive experience with Dr. Weissman's "Tuning Fork" exercise. It cut an energetic chord that was tied between my parents' angst and me, which was instantly liberating. Parents have shared stories of feeling lighter, less reactive, and more compassionate — both with their families and with themselves.

Want to go deeper? You can explore Dr. Weissman's step-by-step support in approaching stressors with love and gratitude, transforming how you show up for yourself and your family. (see TheLifelineCenter.com)

RELEASE PTSD WITH EMDR: EYE MOVEMENT DESENSITIZING AND REPROCESSING

Eye Movement Desensitization and Reprocessing (EMDR) is more straightforward than it sounds. It can benefit parents who often juggle daily stress while carrying old hurts that resurface in unexpected ways, such as snapping at a child's question or feeling panicked by a harmless question or a perceived slight. EMDR is designed to help you process memories and reactions, so they no longer have a grip on your present.

This therapy utilizes bilateral stimulation, such as moving your eyes side to side or tapping your hands, while you briefly focus on a disturbing memory. You don't need to relive every detail, just enough to notice how it feels in your body. Over time, those emotions soften.

There's strong science behind EMDR, which leading health organizations recommend for treating trauma and PTSD. Some people notice their triggers lose intensity after a few sessions. You may experience fewer emotional flashbacks and greater patience during family chaos with this system.

EMDR isn't only for severe trauma. Even stressful events, such as a harsh breakup, a financial setback, or repeated criticism, can create patterns that EMDR helps unwind. You might notice, after working with a trained professional, that heated arguments with your partner or child don't push the same buttons as before.

The therapy is structured and safe. Each session is guided by a therapist who keeps you grounded and checks in often about your comfort level. EMDR has helped parents feel lighter, sleep better, and respond to conflict with a clarity that they didn't know was possible. (see EMDRconsulting.com for free worksheets)

LET A CRANIAL NERVE CHANGE YOUR RESPONSES TO TRIGGERS, OVERWHELM, AND INFLAMMATION

When life feels chaotic, the vagus nerve offers a way to calm your body and mind. Running from the brain to the organs, the vagus nerve is the 10th and longest cranial nerve —the healing nerve of the body —and a key component of the parasympathetic nervous system. It plays a vital role in regulating many involuntary bodily functions, including heart rate, digestion, and respiratory rate.

The vagus nerve acts as a two-way communication superhighway between the brain and various organs, transmitting sensory information from the body to the brain, heart, lungs, gut, and other organs, and then carrying commands from the brain back to these organs and the nervous system.

Think of your nervous system as having two gears:

Parasympathetic gear is the state of calm, rest-and-digest, repair, and healing.

Sympathetic gear is the fight-flight-freeze state of stress, anxiety, and cravings.

Being stuck in the sympathetic gear is when anger issues appear. It also impairs digestion, immunity, hormone balance, and cognitive function, including memory.

How do you get unstuck from the anger gear and shift into the peace and healing gear? Pharmaceutical companies may not want you to know this. Parasympathetic activation through the vagus nerve is a med-free way to move from a stressed, survival brain state. In a calm state, you can replace limiting habits with better ones, release childhood trauma, and reset your nervous system for radiant health, without meeting resistance from a stressed brain.

** Important: Do not stop taking prescription drugs without discussing this with your medical doctor.*

Shifting gears from the sympathetic to the parasympathetic state is akin to possessing a superpower that enables the management of anger with love, yielding lasting results. How do you shift gears?

Think of the vagus nerve as an internal switch with a unique ability to shift from a stressed, reactive state into one of rest, healing, and connection in which love, peace, and health thrive. How do you flip the inner switch?

Imagine a trusted person's gentle voice instantly soothing you. This is the vagus nerve at work. It tunes into vocal tones, senses safety or threat, and helps your brain decide how to respond.

ACTIVATE YOUR CRUCIAL CRANIAL NERVE: TOOLS AND TECHNIQUES

Through **neuroception,** your nervous system constantly scans for signals from others. This ancient wiring is adaptable due to **neuroplasticity**, which lets you train your brain and the crucial vagus nerve to react differently over time.

Deep breathing can activate the vagus nerve. A deep inhale speeds up your heart rate. A long, slow exhale, accompanied by a vocal sigh, tells your brain and nervous system that you're safe. Aaahhhh.

Can an inflamed temper increase body inflammation? Yes, until the vagus nerve releases an anti-inflammatory neurotransmitter called **acetylcholine.** The sound of an angry shout spikes your heart rate, until a soothing hum slows it, thanks to your vagus nerve. How?

Vocal sound vibrations stimulate vagus nerve fibers in the throat and chest. Simple actions, such as humming, singing, or slow chanting, popularized by **Jim Donovan and the Donovan Health Sound Solu-**

tion, gently activate the vagus nerve. You might invite your children to join you in these activities. (see donovanhealth.com)

You and your family may also be curious to see how electrical stimulation devices, such as the Neubie and The Neurological Fitness Method by Garrett Salpeter, use tiny energy currents to reset vagal tone, retrain stress responses, and support neurological fitness throughout the body for peak performance and injury recovery. This is becoming popular for at-home use. (see neu.fit).

Or consider **Truvaga Plus,** a hand-held electrical stimulation device that is used exclusively to reset the vagal nerve. (see truvaga.com)

Other easy practices to activate the vagus nerve include exhaling slowly with a long sigh, gargling, laughing, tapping, chewing gum, practicing gratitude, singing a favorite song, or splashing cold water on your face for 20 seconds. These practices can help shift your body quickly from a sympathetic state of panic to a parasympathetic state of peace. This is an incentive to laugh out loud, exhale slowly with a long sigh, sing a favorite song with your family, and express gratitude freely as part of your daily routine.

Psychology Today's 9-part series, The Vagus Nerve Survival Guide, which combats fight-or-flight urges, reports that stimulating the vagus nerve can also influence oxytocin release. This love-bonding hormone plays a role in mood regulation, social bonding, and the gut-brain connection. (see APA List: 98)

The presence of the bonding hormone oxytocin automatically reduces your body's cortisol levels. Similarly, the presence of high-vibrating emotions like love and gratitude that you nurture through exercises here automatically reduces levels of low-vibrating emotions such as anger and fear in the fight-or-flight survival state. In this philosophical framework, the highest mental and emotional vibration always wins by attracting high-vibrational people, experiences, and circumstances.

Now you empower your vagus nerve to shift from a state of anger or anxiety to one of calm and peace, by exploring these exercises.

DIVE INTO AN ICY, FULL-BODY STATE OF PARASYMPATHETIC CALM EXERCISE

Try the Popular Polar Bear Plunge. You can immerse your whole body, including your head, in ice-cold water, such as a wintry lake, an ice-water tank, or a freezing shower. This triggers a "Dive Reflex" that lowers your heart rate and instantly shifts your body into a parasympathetic calm state.

Start with 30 to 60 seconds and gradually work up to 5 minutes, depending on your tolerance. It's crucial to listen to your body and get out of the cold if you begin to feel dizzy, experience numbness, or start shivering.

SHIFT INTO PARASYMPATHETIC CALM WITH A BDNF LIFT USING HEAT EXERCISE

Research shows that heating your entire body in a 10 to 15-minute sauna or a comfortably hot shower boosts **BDNF,** your brain's "grow and repair" chemical. Be sure to drink pure water before and after, to stay hydrated as you heat up and cool down.

What does the science say? After heat, your body shifts toward the "rest and digest" state, and heart rate patterns show more parasympathetic activity —the peaceful side of your nervous system.

Another benefit: The brain's **"BDNF Lift"** lasts up to an hour after heat exposure, so it's smart to devote that hour to do focused work, like studying or practicing your favorite techniques that you're exploring here, while your brain is primed to wire in new skills.

What if you want to reap the benefits of a BDNF Lift on learning and sleep on the same day? Try heating your body a couple of hours before bedtime, do your focused practice or study right after, and then give yourself an hour to relax before sleep. (see APA List: 42, 43, 44)

STIMULATE THE LONGEST CRANIAL NERVE WITH AN EYE EXERCISE

This simple eye exercise stimulates your longest cranial nerve--the vagus nerve. In a seated position for safety, slowly circle your eyes clockwise, making two complete rotations. Then reverse direction. Slowly circle your eyes counterclockwise, making two complete rotations. Celebrate this small win with a smile. Smiling also stimulates the vagus nerve.

Over time, restoring healthy vagus nerve function builds resilience, enabling you to recover more quickly from anger and overwhelm, and to respond to stressors more effectively and sleep better. (see APA list: 41)

ENERGIZE BRAIN FITNESS WITH A LEADING-EDGE TECHNOLOGY: THE BRAIN TAP SYSTEM

Some days, it feels like your mind is racing in a hundred directions. You're juggling work, meals, school forms, and the constant chatter of family life. When my energy dips and my focus drifts, especially during that mid-afternoon slump, the Brain Tap Headset becomes my reset button. This isn't just another gadget collecting dust on a shelf.

Brain Tap, a guided audiovisual system developed and narrated by Dr Patrick Porter, weaves together five cutting-edge technologies to help your brain shift gears and find balance. Light frequencies gently pulse through closed eyelids, syncing with your body's natural rhythms.

Meanwhile, auriculotherapy targets specific points on the ears known to influence stress levels and mood. Beats and tones work in harmony with guided visualizations, creating a soundscape that nudges you toward relaxation, clarity, or even deep sleep, depending on your needs. The addition of 10 Cycle Holographic Music offers a rich, layered experience that soothes mental noise and helps you recharge quickly.

I appreciate how easily Brain Tap sessions can be integrated into everyday life. In ten or twenty minutes with my headset on, I relax as the system does its work. I don't need any special skills on my part. I emerge sharper, refreshed, and ready to leap all the hurdles the rest of the day may present.

Research supports the use of these sensory tools for balancing brain waves, promoting healing from stress, enhancing learning, supporting recovery from addiction, and facilitating restorative sleep. For parents who crave more energy and mental clarity without endless caffeine intake, this approach feels like a gentle nudge back to balance. It's a high-tech form of self-care that achieves the rapid results you want in a busy day. (see braintap.com)

UNLOCK THE POWER OF A QUANTUM TOOL FOR FAMILY HARMONY

Imagine standing at a crossroads when family tension is at its highest. Do you react out of old patterns? Or could you access a different, more harmonious version of yourself?

Quantum Jumping, a concept popularized by the late Burt Goldman, offers an imaginary yet powerful experience for parents who crave change but feel stuck.

Here's the core idea: There are many possible "You's" in the quantum field, each living slightly different lives. By tapping into the mindset of one of these alternate selves — perhaps the one who handles conflict calmly or laughs more easily — you may merge it into your real life. This lets your imagination open energetic pathways to healthier habits. How do you give this a try?

Picture a specific challenge, such as sibling rivalry that disrupts peace in the car or a recurring disagreement with your teenager that triggers tension at dinner. Close your eyes. Imagine a "Quantum You" who navigates this moment with grace, patience, and even humor. What does this version of you say? How do they stand, breathe, and respond? The mind's ability to visualize new possibilities actually can rewire neural pathways, making new calm responses feel less foreign and more accessible.

You may notice a ripple effect. As you shift, your child mirrors you. You may enrich many aspects of life, health, and relationships with **Quantum Jumping audiovisualizations guided by Burt Goldman.** (see mindvalley.com)

All you need to start is 10 to 20 minutes of quiet and a willingness to try something new. Quantum Jumping enables you to break cycles and step into healthier family dynamics, sometimes with instant results. When anger moves in, close your eyes and "jump" into the calmest version of yourself you can imagine. Merge their wisdom with yours. Open your eyes. Try out their approach for real.

UNLEASH THE POWER OF YOUR HEART TO HEAL ANGER

HeartMath utilizes the concept of the heart's intelligence and its ability to influence brain and emotional states to help transform depleting emotions, such as anger, into more energizing ones, like love, compassion, gratitude, and joy.

HeartMath doesn't literally "heal anger with love" in the sense of a magic cure. It empowers us to cultivate positive emotional states that help reduce the intensity and duration of anger, as well as its detrimental effects on family health.

Here's how HeartMath relates to "Healing anger with love":

- **Heart-Brain Communication:** HeartMath emphasizes the scientific understanding that the heart possesses its own complex nervous system, AKA "the brain in the heart," that communicates with the brain in the head.
- **Heart Rhythm Patterns:** Different emotional states are associated with distinct heart rhythm patterns. Stressful emotions, like anger and envy, create chaotic and disordered patterns (incoherent). Positive emotions, such as appreciation and love, make smooth, harmonious patterns (coherence).

- **Transforming Emotions:** By consciously generating positive feelings and achieving heart rhythm coherence, we can influence our physiological state and transform negative emotions. This transformation enables a shift from anger and frustration to more positive, adaptive responses.
- **Techniques and Tools:** HeartMath offers specific tools, such as the "Freeze-Frame" and the "Cut-Thru" techniques, to help achieve heart coherence and regulate emotions. (see heartmath.org/freeze-frame/)
- **Forgiveness and Love:** HeartMath also emphasizes the role of forgiveness in releasing negative emotions and restoring well-being. Cultivating forgiveness, kindness, and love through heart-focused practices can contribute to emotional healing and enriched interactions in parent-child relationships.

What does science say? Your emotional energy matters. Your heart generates the strongest electromagnetic field in your body. Emotions such as love, compassion, joy, and gratitude harmonize the heart-brain interaction, enhancing emotional regulation and immune response, raising your energetic frequency, and attracting people and experiences of higher frequencies, since like attracts like vibrationally. (see heartmath.com/science/#)

GO FROM FEELING TERROR TO CALM TECHNIQUES AND EXERCISES

Have you ever experienced a Night Terror? You bolt upright from a deep sleep. Your heart pumps faster. You may recall a dream fragment that terrified you. Or perhaps an unknown terror scared you half to death. This is when intentional breathing becomes your lifeline. How?

Slow, deep breaths flip a switch in your body, activating the parasympathetic nervous system that tells your brain and heart, "It's safe to let go."

TAKE TWO MINUTES FOR A LETTING GO EXERCISE

Breathe in love with every cell of your body. In a long exhale with an audible sigh, breathe out fear from every cell. Repeat the exercise by breathing out anger from every cell with a loud sigh and by breathing in through your nose all the love that's present. How many repetitions will it take for you to feel anger loosen its grip?

FIND THE CALM IN CHAOS TECHNIQUES

No extra time is needed to tap into the power of your breath.

Box breathing is simple. Inhale for four counts, hold for four, exhale for four, hold for four. Just a minute of repetition brings surprising clarity and calm. Increase benefits by inhaling for 20 counts, holding a breath for 20 counts, and exhaling for 20 counts.

Alternate nostril breathing can sharpen focus and soothe frazzled nerves. Gently close one nostril, inhale. Switch sides and exhale. Repeat two cycles.

Both techniques may be practiced while waiting for water to boil, so you don't need to schedule time for it. You can weave breathwork into your daily transitions, such as during your commute, while brushing your teeth, or as a nightly wind-down before bed. Children love joining in, especially if you pretend to blow up balloons or make dragon breaths together.

TEACH YOUR CHILD THE NOSE TO TOES EMPOWERMENT EXERCISE

Show your child how breathing through their nose can calm and empower them, while simultaneously wiggling their toes can ground them in the present moment when all is well and as it should be. This exercise helps them remain calm in stressful situations.

Over time, regular breathwork can change the energy in a household. Children learn that feelings don't control them, that they can guide their breath, and that they can choose calm over chaos. As you model this, you make emotional self-regulation seem like a straightforward way to find quiet in a chaotic day.

ENHANCE YOUR DAILY HEALTH HABITS TO HELP MANAGE ANGER WITH LOVE

Have you ever eaten a bag of cookies or chips while watching TV? You quickly learned how your food choices can impact how you feel. Eating processed snacks or skipping meals can cause your blood sugar to skyrocket, then plummet. Quick spikes are followed by crashes, often leaving you irritable or anxious. Balanced meals that combine healthy carbohydrates, protein, and fats help keep blood sugar levels steady, making emotions more stable in children and adults.

Low levels of vital nutrients, such as magnesium and B vitamins, often manifest as impatience, trouble focusing, and an "off" feeling. Low iron levels can leave you feeling tired and irritable. Not getting enough omega-3s, found in foods such as salmon, walnuts, and chia seeds, may dull your mood or make stress management more difficult. Spinach, avocados, and pumpkin seeds are rich in magnesium, which can help you relax. (see APA List: 19)

You don't need elaborate meals to eat well. Simple meal prep, such as washing vegetables, boiling eggs, or cooking a batch of brown rice or quinoa on the weekends, saves time and makes nutritious choices easier during busy weeks. Swap sugary cereals for sprouted oatmeal with plain yogurt and berries. Carry nuts and fruit instead of candy bars for quick snacks.

Hydration is just as crucial for maintaining a good mood. Even if you're mildly dehydrated, you can feel anger, brain fog, and fatigue. It's important to drink purified water whenever possible to avoid microplastics and forever chemicals detected in tap water.

A Newsweek article (9-25-25) reported that three cancer-causing chemicals were detected in tap water that nearly 100 million Americans drink, suggesting that our public drinking water treatment systems can be updated to treat multiple contaminants simultaneously. (see APA list: 78)

Drinking a glass of purified water before your morning coffee keeps you hydrated. When a child gets cranky, offer water first because children and adults often confuse thirst with hunger.

Avoid Artificial Sweeteners (AS) to protect brain health. In a Brazilian study published in the October 7, 2025 issue of **NEUROLOGY,** among 12,772 adult participants, those who consumed the most artificial sweeteners had "significantly faster declines" in thinking and memory skills. While the eight-year study showed a link between the use of some artificial sweeteners and cognitive decline, it did not prove that artificial sweeteners were the cause. (see APA list: 47) Are you willing to take that risk with your brain health?

Why is it wise to nourish and protect your brain from toxins as you manage anger with love? Because you're counting on your brain's neuroplasticity to grow new brain cells and form new neural pathways that make parasympathetic peace your new normal brain state, in which love thrives and anger fades.

Clear Stored Waste from Your Digestive Tract Before It Taints Your Mood. Does your gut actually influence your mood?

"An angry gut can make for a moody and anxious mind," claims Dr. David Perlmutter in his book, BRAIN MAKER. How do you create a happy gut? Consider increasing your exposure to beneficial bacteria that promote gut and brain health, found in fermented foods, plain yogurt, or a lab-tested multi-strain probiotic supplement.

You also want to limit your exposure to harmful bacteria associated with bad moods. Research shows that sugar feeds unhealthy gut bacteria, so avoiding sugar-laden foods like soda, candy, cookies, cake, and ice cream may help lower levels of nasty bugs, allowing beneficial bacteria to thrive while supporting a happy gut and mood. (see APA list: 58)

Let's apply the "happy gut" theory to the longevity secrets of the world's oldest person. In 2024, a Spanish woman named Maria Branyas Morera died in her sleep at age 117, without any chronic health issues. Maria's secrets to healthy longevity? She enjoyed gardening, sleeping, reading books, taking walks, spending time with friends, playing the piano, having dogs, and eating three plain yogurts each day. That daily dose of probiotics may be how Maria increased the beneficial bacteria in her microbiome, promoting a healthy gut and a happy brain throughout her 117 years of life. Maria's daily movement and connection with friends are also linked to healthy longevity.

Are you curious about the balance of good and bad bugs in your microbiome? Will you consider doing an at-home microbiome test? Then you'll receive a custom list of foods and drinks that feed your good bacteria and good moods. (see viome.com)

You can also enhance the gut-brain connection by clearing the waste that's stuck in your digestive tract, using the botanical protocols that I've relied on for decades.

Master herbalist, Dr. Richard Schulze, has been leading the natural health revolution since 1970. He recommends five steps that can change your life:

1. Boost energy with powerful nutrition.
2. Eliminate stored toxic waste.
3. Build a strong immune system.
4. Perform regular preventive maintenance for your entire body.
5. Fix a little problem before it becomes a big problem, much like you would for your car to keep it tuned up and running smoothly.

Your digestive tract is as long as two SUVs parked head to tail. You want to clear out the stuck waste, so it can't poison you and your mood from the inside. You also want to consume premium fuel each day to support resilient health and happiness. Dr. Schulze guides you through the process in a gift catalogue of his protocols, which you may download from his website. (see herbdoc.com)

MINIMIZE EXPOSURE TO SNEAKY THREATS WHICH SUPPRESS EMOTIONAL REGULATION, PARTICULARLY IN CHILDREN

The world today is full of invisible stressors. Many come not from work or relationships, but from the environment itself. Chemicals and toxins can be found in unexpected places, including cleaning sprays, plastic food containers, plastic toothbrush bristles, plastic chewing gum base, fabric softeners, and air fresheners that provide a powerful scent boost.

Children's developing brains and bodies are susceptible to these sneaky threats. When a child is exposed to substances like **The Five Ps- -Phthalates, Parabens, Pesticides, PFAS, and Plastics**--studies show that their ability to regulate emotions can be compromised. You might notice more tantrums, anxiety, or sleep struggles, without ever connecting these issues to what's in a child's environment.

Adults aren't immune to harm from exposure to The Five P's, which **Dr. Jack Wolfson, the author of The Paleo Cardiologist**, claims are linked to heart attacks, heart disease, hormone disruption, and strokes. (see APA list: 19)

Should dementia be added to Dr. Wolfson's list? A **2025 study by the University of New Mexico** detected high levels of microplastics in the brains of 52 people who died with dementia. (see APA list: 63, 64)

Although microplastics in the brain aren't claimed to be the direct cause of dementia in this study, do you want to risk your brain health by ingesting microplastics contained in packaged foods, tap water, seafood, chewing gum, oral and body-care products, etc.?

I won't accept that potential health risk, which is why I'm suggesting healthier alternatives for you to consider now.

MAKE A BIG DIFFERENCE IN YOUR MOOD AND HEALTH BY MAKING SMALL SHIFTS

Swap out plastic water bottles for copper (once used in home water pipes), glass, or stainless steel.

Explore a home reverse osmosis system that removes 99.99% of microplastics, forever chemicals, heavy metals, parasites, and other contaminants detected in tap water, remineralizing the drinking water to an ideal pH level.

Consider bamboo-bristle toothbrushes to replace plastic ones that feed you microplastics each time you brush.

Select bamboo-based toilet paper that is free of formaldehyde, bleach, and many chemicals used to process toilet paper made from trees. Choosing bamboo is also a sustainable alternative that saves trees.

Choose a chewing gum that has a plastic-free gum base, which is also free of artificial sweeteners.

Look for fragrance-free and dye-free laundry detergents, like Miracle II Liquid Soap. My grown children tease me about using Miracle II on everything, much like the Mom in *My Big Fat Greek Wedding*, who spritzes glass cleaner on everything. It's true. I love using Miracle II as a laundry detergent/fabric softener, for mopping floors, for luxurious bubble baths, and for bathing the dog and the car. It's potent yet pure enough for a baby to drink, although that's not recommended.

Make safe cleaning mixtures with vinegar, baking soda, and lemon, helping you keep harsh fumes out of your home and your body.

Look for the word "Fragrance" on an ingredient list. If you spot it, think twice. "Fragrance" often hides dozens of untested chemicals.

Consider investing in a HEPA air filter if you live in a city, near busy roads, or have a pet at home. HEPA-filtered air in the bedroom lets you breathe 99.9% pure air while you sleep, ideally for 7-8 hours each night.

Get rid of toys that can be culprits. Choose wooden or cloth options over cheap colored plastics, especially for a young child who puts everything in their mouth.

Shop for skincare products with fewer ingredients, which usually means fewer risks.

Be mindful of this: What you lather on your skin may end up in your bloodstream. Be careful of hair dyes that soak your scalp for the same reason.

I love using body creams made from rich organic, food-grade oils, fruits, and veggies. When you bring safer products into your home, you may help stabilize your child's mood and allow yourself to breathe a little easier, while you manage anger with love, like you are being guided to do here.

GUESS WHICH 5 TOXINS HARM RELATIONSHIPS. GET THE ANTIDOTES

You don't eat, drink, inhale, or lather on these toxins. You can harm relationships with five toxic actions and attitudes:

1. Raging Prevents Managing Anger With Love
2. Complaining Prevents Embracing Productive Change
3. Criticizing Prevents Expressing Love And Gratitude
4. Punishing Harshly Prevents Inspiring The Best
5. Blaming Prevents Empowering Self-Growth

Now reverse the results by reading the action on the right first, then reading the word "prevents", stating the action on the left.

As you eliminate from your life the five toxic actions and attitudes on the left using the practical tools explored in each chapter, you start doing what works to boost mood and health and stop doing what doesn't. This personal growth has a cascading impact on your family, driven by the ripple effect of emotional contagion.

You will foster greater growth in yourself and your family by implementing your preferred strategies from among these exercises:

SUPPORT EMOTIONAL REGULATION EXERCISES

Break a stress spiral with a quick burst of movement. When you move your body —whether walking briskly with your dog, dancing in the kitchen, or holding a five-minute plank challenge —your brain releases endorphins. These are your body's natural mood boosters, and they kick in quickly.

Exercise also lowers cortisol, the stress hormone that makes you feel on edge. That's why even a short jog or a few yoga stretches can leave you feeling lighter. Regular movement strengthens muscles, keeps joints limber, moves lymph fluid, and burns off the kind of fat that can store toxins. Over time, you'll notice fewer aches and a calmer mood. You can achieve these benefits without running a marathon, which can cause your body to "hit the wall."

What does the science say? Recent neuroscience studies report that even gentle exercise can enhance your brain's plasticity by forming new brain cells over time, thereby improving brain function and mood. (see ASA list: 40)

Yoga and Tai Chi promote a healthy mind-body connection by combining deep breathing with gentle stretches, allowing you to improve flexibility and focus simultaneously. Cardio activities, such as playing tennis or tag with your children, can help strengthen your heart while you blow off steam. You can work out at home while the baby naps, or do squats in the bathroom before your shower. Tiny bursts still count. Stretching as a team before bed is a routine that relaxes you into sleep.

TRY A FIFTEEN-MINUTE POST-MEAL FAMILY EXERCISE

A family walk or bike ride for fifteen minutes after a meal helps move food through the digestive tract, moves lymph fluid (which lacks a pump to propel its flow), and promotes family bonding in a shared activity.

When you move together as a family, something shifts. Laughter bubbles up. Fights fade out. Also, organize weekend soccer games or dance contests to bring everyone together and create a sense of community. These moments build connection and make you feel part of the home team, rather than just a group of weary people under one roof.

CLEAR ANGER ENERGY THAT'S STUCK IN A VITAL ORGAN, UTILIZING TWO ANCIENT EXERCISES

Emotions are energy in motion. In Traditional Chinese Medicine (TCM), QiGong exercises are used to move and clear anger energy that's trapped in the liver by regulating the flow of "Qi" (vital energy).

Symptoms of stagnant liver "Qi" can include irritability, mood swings, headaches, and physical tension. Try releasing stagnant liver Qi with two ancient exercises:

PUNCH THE AIR REPEATEDLY WITH A FOCUSED, ANGRY GAZE EXERCISE

This vigorous punching movement helps release stuck anger and frustration energy that's associated with the liver.

SOOTHE THE LIVER AND CLEAR STUCK ANGER ENERGY EXERCISE

Rub your palms together 60 times to warm your palm energy. Place both palms over your liver, which is on the right side under your ribs. Close your eyes. Imagine someone you love deeply who fully opens your heart. Feel love energy moving from your heart, through your hands, and into your liver. Feel love's high frequency replace anger's low frequency as you breathe in love and exhale anger, mentally saying, "The highest frequency always wins."

Want an extra boost? Rub your palms together for another 30 seconds. Place your palms on your lowest right rib. Scoop upward, pulling anger energy out of the liver. Then flick anger energy from your hands into the earth. Do this exercise as needed to release the energetic claws of anger.

What does the science say? While TCM principles linking emotions to organs differ from those in Western medicine, research suggests that QiGong is effective in reducing stress and promoting emotional regulation, thereby enhancing overall well-being. (see APA list: 48)

** Always consult a healthcare professional before starting a new protocol. If you're struggling with health, anxiety, or depression, please consult a licensed professional. Your mind is powerful. So is traditional medical care. The information provided is educational; it's not medical advice.*

CREATE A SOOTHING ZEN ZONE AT HOME

Imagine a space in your home where stress melts away. It's a valid Zen Zone. This isn't just a reading and nap nook. It's a dedicated area designed to help you decompress and soothe nerves on a hectic day. A Zen Zone signals to your mind and body, "You can let go here." Even a chair by a window or a corner with floor cushions can activate a calming response.

Begin by choosing soothing colors, such as soft blues, warm grays, or muted earth tones, to lower tension. Consider adding a serene soundtrack featuring sounds of rainforest birds, wildlife, waterfalls, and gentle rain. **Gentle sounds of nature are "Glimmers" that cue your brain and nervous system to feel safe.**

Ask your child to choose an aromatherapy scent and string up mini lights for a soft glow in the family's sacred space, where you will retreat to rest and refresh.

"CAST YOUR BURDEN" EXERCISE

It Works Well When Practiced Often, Because Practice Makes Permanent.

I sought a permanent release of the shattering shock waves I felt after the SEC notified me that my life savings had been stolen in a securities investment brokered by two advisors whom I thought I could trust.

The traumatic aftershocks of their theft seized my focus at least 50 times a day at first and kept me in an acute fight, flight, and freeze response of terror. My son gave me wise guidance, suggesting I review **The Wisdom of Florence Scovel Shinn: 4 Complete Books**, (see APA list: 75), select a technique that resonates with me, and practice it regularly until it becomes effective for me (much like I ask you to choose techniques in this book and work with them until they become effective for you).

I chose a technique called "Casting the Burden." It releases heavy emotional loads and worries by entrusting them to a higher power, often referred to as the Christ within. Depending on your spiritual tradition, feel free to substitute these synonyms —the deeper self, the atman, or the Buddha Nature —for the Christ within as you say this script out loud or silently to yourself.

Florence Scovel Shinn's script: **"I cast the burden of (name your burden) on (name your higher power/deeper self), and I go free."**

Here's how I tweaked my script: **"I cast the burden of loss and lack on the Christ within, and I go free. I give thanks for my abundance and prosperity, which I'm divinely entitled to savor and share with joy. Thank you for all my blessings and lessons. Thank you for letting me be an instrument of your love."**

I practiced Casting the Burden each time the shocking reality of this life-altering theft gripped my throat and stole my breath throughout the day and night. After a couple of months of daily practice, while I was stuck in the initial shock and denial stage of grief, this devastating burden was lifted. I'm thankful I was able to let go of this burden before I reached the second stage of grief, which is anger.

Casting the Burden helped me avoid the ravaging impact that anger over loss can have on the heart and health. I'm thankful that Casting the Burden helped me leap over the subsequent grief stages that follow anger, which include bargaining and depression, because I did the emotional work that helped me jump to the final stage of grief, which is acceptance. (see APA list: 45)

Casting the Burden throughout the day changed the trajectory of my life after loss. It shifted my mindset from a state of fight, flight, and freeze to a calm one, where I accepted my new action plan to take charge of my financial life and reclaim my sense of emotional safety and security. How does this practice work?

ENERGIZE THE SUBCONSCIOUS MIND TO WORK FOR YOU, NOT AGAINST YOU

The act of casting the burden is believed to impress the subconscious mind with a sense of release, raising the energetic vibration and attracting positive, higher-frequency experiences. It's the universal law of attraction in action. Here are highlights of the process.

First, you think of an outcome you want and feel enthusiastic gratitude for it, as if you already have it. Don't just think of the outcome; fall in love with it.

Your thoughts generate electrical energy. Your emotions (like feeling love and gratitude) give it frequency. This frequency attracts outcomes of the same frequency. It's like tuning into a favorite radio program. When you want to listen to it, you need to take action. You change the channel to access the program that is on your wavelength. Why bother?

You are what you are aware of. You attract what you are, not what you want or lack. Like attracts like energetically when you take the right action. The action I kept taking was casting the burden until I no longer carried its weight. This tool worked for me because I put in the effort. I also needed additional tools and a new action plan to rebuild the economic security that was stolen from me. I could have found a trustworthy investment advisor if I had taken the time to look for one. Instead, I trusted myself. I decided to earn several securities licenses to learn how to rebuild, grow, and protect my financial safety net.

What other lessons did I learn from this life-changing challenge? I learned resilient people don't ask, "Why me?" They ask, "What can I learn from this? In shifting my perspective from grieving a 7-figure loss to finding the lessons in it, I realized no one escapes loss and its challenges. We will all be tested as a catalyst for a life-transforming breakthrough. We can choose to resist the test, which was my initial reaction, which caused intense pain in every fiber of my being.

Alternatively, a more enlightened approach that bypasses the pain is to immediately give thanks for the test as an initial reaction, even for the test that changes the trajectory of our lives. What does giving thanks for a test sound like?

While facing a great test, say to yourself: "All is well. Everything is working out for my highest good. Out of this situation, only good will come, and I am safe." Will you repeat it as often as required to restore calm? (credit: Louise Hay)

I have room to grow toward a more enlightened approach, yet at least I'm on the path. That may be why my daughter has tenderly called me "Dalai Mama."

I've shared the story of this financial setback to illustrate how the power of resilience, lifelong learning, and the holistic, quantum toolkit that you're exploring here can be leveraged to achieve even more. This includes managing anger with love, healing triggers, and teaching by example how to build emotional intelligence in happy relationships.

Your willingness to take new actions and use new tools to get new results empowers you to transform even a traumatic crisis into a personal triumph.

As your child sees you bounce back and grow through a crisis, they learn that resilience is a skill that helps you recover from any setback. You also teach by example that authentic wealth can be built, but it can't be stolen. Why? Because building authentic wealth that enriches your life and your relationships with others and yourself is an inside job, much like the pursuit you're undertaking here.

In the next chapter, you will take a deeper dive into the proven tools that elevate your actions and interactions in every aspect of life. But first...

PAUSE TO MAKE A DIFFERENCE AND UNLOCK THE POWER OF GENEROSITY WITH YOUR REVIEW

Giving and receiving are interconnected aspects of the flow of communication and energy, fostering abundance through acts of kindness and sharing.

People who give without expecting anything in return live happier lives. So, let's make a difference together.

Will you help a parent just like you—curious about how to manage anger with love but unsure where to start? You've already reached the mid-point of your journey through our practical guidebook, anticipating many golden insights ahead.

My mission is to make *ANGER MANAGEMENT FOR PARENTS* available to every parent who wants more love and fewer fights, so they can be the best parent and partner they can be now.

Since I want to reach more parents, I'd like your help.

Most people choose books based on reviews. So, I'm asking you to help a fellow parent who wants to manage anger with love by leaving a review.

It costs nothing and takes a minute, yet it could spark a parent's journey from a stressed survival brain state into a calm state where love thrives. Your review could help another parent begin their journey to heal triggers and raise confident, caring children in happy relationships.

How do you make a difference now?

Scan QR CODE:

Or copy and paste this URL into your browser:

https://amazon.com/review/review-your-purchases/?asin=
B0GR5F2711

Then take a minute to leave a review.

I thank you, and I wish you love.
Hadley Finch

CHAPTER 6
THE POWER OF EFFECTIVE COMMUNICATION

ACTIVE LISTENING: A DEEPER EXPLORATION OF THIS KEY TO UNDERSTANDING

FAMILY COMMUNICATION IS BEYOND WORDS. It may be a sigh, a glance, or a shrug that says more than a whole speech. Imagine coming home after a long, loud day. The house is buzzing. A child negotiates playtime, a partner scrolls their phone, and the dog barks for food. You ask your child how school went, and they shrug and say, "Fine." You sense there's more beneath the surface, but you're tired and distracted. It's easy to nod and move on, yet important messages are lost when no one truly listens.

Active listening can transform the entire atmosphere of your home. It means putting away your phone, making eye contact, and giving your child your full attention in that moment. The reward is getting info about their day and sending a message that they matter to you.

Active listening is the secret sauce behind strong parent-child bonds. At its core, it's not about hearing words as much as giving your complete focus and showing, with your whole presence, that you care. You aren't waiting for your turn to talk or planning your response as they speak. You are soaking up every word and gesture. Maintaining eye contact is a powerful signal that tells your child, "You have my attention." For little ones, it helps to kneel, so you're on their level. For older children and teens, a gentle gaze works wonders. Nodding as they talk is another subtle yet effective cue. Your child will notice that you're tracking with them. This boosts their confidence to keep sharing, as you're creating a safe space for mutual understanding.

How do you practice active listening? You need to do more than look and nod. Reflecting the gist of what your child says is a game-changer.

If your son complains about losing at soccer and storms off, you might say, "Sounds like you're pretty upset about the game." You don't jump to fix a problem or give advice, which doesn't work. Your quiet presence, along with active listening, works. You show them you understand how they feel. This reflection helps a child process their emotions and learn to trust their voice.

You can begin by asking open-ended questions that will invite more sharing. "What was the hardest part?" and "How did that make you feel?" require more than "Yes" or "No" responses. Open-ended questions encourage your child to explore their thoughts with you. Resist the urge to interrupt or share your own stories right away. Listen, reflect, and ask gentle follow-ups. Even if there's a silent pause, let it breathe. A child may need a moment to find their words.

Active listening has a ripple effect on family relationships. When children feel heard, emotional walls come down. You'll notice fewer power struggles and more cooperation when children sense that their opinions count.

Practicing active listening with your partner and/or co-parent can transform tense exchanges into more productive conversations, helping to fulfill the goal of knowing and being known in your relationship.

Instead of arguing over an issue, get curious, not furious. Reflect the gist of what the other person says. "Are you feeling overwhelmed by the mess in the living room?" This can lower their guard and bypass blame. Forming these habits fosters trust, enabling your entire family to speak up without fear of being dismissed or misunderstood.

Real-life examples show how active listening makes a difference. First, picture a classic sibling argument over who gets to use the tablet first. You walk in to find voices raised and tears threatening. Instead of ordering everyone to quiet down or picking sides, you kneel between them and ask each child to explain what happened, one at a time. You look them in the eyes, nod, and repeat back what they say. "So you wanted a turn because you were waiting all afternoon." "And you felt upset because you thought it was your turn."

As each child feels understood, anger drains away bit by bit. They may start negotiating on their own, even offering solutions you hadn't thought of. All you did was listen for deeper meanings and reflect on what you heard. This develops self-driven problem-solving and a sense of fairness in your child.

Now, imagine an adult scenario, such as a rough patch with your partner after a busy week. Perhaps there's tension over forgotten errands or missed events. Instead of jumping straight to accusations ("You never help out"), try sitting down together after the children are asleep. Maintain eye contact, put away distractions, and allow each of you to speak uninterrupted for a few minutes. Your partner says something like, "I feel invisible because nobody sees my effort." Instead of countering with your complaints, reflect on your view of what they said. "You're feeling unappreciated lately." Their moment of being heard may soften a hard edge and reveal a path to real solutions, less distance, and deeper understanding.

REFLECT ON ACTIVE LISTENING EXERCISE

Take three days this week and choose one conversation each day with your child (or partner) to practice active listening.

- Put away all distractions.
- Maintain steady eye contact.
- Nod or show with your face that you're engaged.
- Reflect what you hear ("So you're saying…").
- Make open-ended requests. ("Tell me more about that").

- Afterward, jot down what changed in the mood or outcome of the conversation. Notice if your child opens up more than usual, if arguments end more quickly, or if problem-solving feels easier.

Active listening isn't complicated, yet it does take conscious effort. The rewards may be fewer misunderstandings, more cooperation, and deeper trust at home. When a child sees that you value their thoughts and feelings, even when those thoughts are messy or inconvenient, they learn to listen more effectively. You're helping a child build a skill that enriches their interactions and creates happy relationships. (see APA list: 29)

VALIDATE YOUR CHILD'S FEELINGS WITH EMPATHY

Let's take a deeper look at how empathy can transform family life. When your child comes to you upset—about a scraped knee, a missing toy, or piles of homework—the most helpful response isn't advice or a quick fix. What matters most is your willingness to show you understand what they're experiencing.

Responding with empathy shows your child that their emotions are valued. You give them space for their feelings and assure them you're on their side. This goes beyond just saying, "I'm sorry you're upset". It's about showing real understanding and respect for how they feel. Validating your child sends a clear message. "Your emotions are safe to share with me."

Empathy evolves from active listening. You listen to your child's words and find meaning beneath them, as you notice their tone and body language. If your daughter slumps at the table, pencil motionless over a math worksheet, you resist the urge to lecture or fix. Instead, you sit beside her, match her tone gently, and say, "This looks hard for you tonight." Phrases like "I see why you feel that way" help your child feel seen and heard. These simple yet powerful words tell your child that you see their struggle, without judgment.

Matching your child's emotional energy, without mirroring their upset exactly, is essential. If your son storms in from school, face flushed with anger, it's tempting to tell him to calm down. Instead, meet his intensity with calm empathy. "Sounds like today was extra tough." You don't need to match anger with anger, or get sad when your child is. Reflect some of their emotional tone. Soften your voice when they're unhappy. Speak gently when they're vulnerable.

Staying quiet with a child while they cry or vent often is enough, because your quiet presence soothes them and speaks volumes.

Communicating with empathy offers lasting benefits. Children who experience empathy from their parents tend to develop greater emotional intelligence. They can name their feelings. They are more comfortable sharing with others. Trust grows. Power struggles diminish. A child will come to you as problems get larger, knowing you'll listen without criticism.

Fostering resilience is another benefit of empathetic communication. When children feel validated, they can better handle setbacks and recover from disappointments. They don't need to act out or escalate to be understood. If your child is upset about a lost friendship, acknowledge the hurt. "Losing a friend is so hard." This comforts them. Telling them to get over it doesn't. Empathetic communication helps build self-esteem when a child knows their feelings are understood and accepted.

What if your eight-year-old is stuck on her math homework and near tears? Instead of saying, "Just try harder," you pause, notice her distress, and say, "Math can be so confusing, especially after a long day." She relaxes and might tell you exactly where she's struggling, making it easier to help and turn the process into a teamwork effort, without conflict.

Another scenario: Your teen comes home after failing a test he studied for. He grumbles and goes to his room. You won't ignore him or get irritated. You won't offer an unwelcome truth, such as "A failure is feedback on what needs your focus." Instead, you gently say, "It sounds like you're feeling disappointed after all that effort." He may not open up right away, but your empathy creates emotional space for future conversations about what to do next.

Even minor disappointments are opportunities for empathy. When your preschooler cries because her sparkly shirt is in the wash, kneel and say, "I know you wanted to wear your favorite shirt." She feels understood and may recover faster than if you'd dismissed her feelings.

Showing empathy is challenging when you're exhausted or overwhelmed. When you pause before speaking and remember that your child's feelings are huge to them, you're likely to respond with an open heart and validate their emotions. This builds a child's trust that they can tell you anything.

TURN CONFLICTS INTO GROWTH OPPORTUNITIES EXERCISES

Conflict is a regular part of family life, yet it doesn't have to mean chaos or hurt feelings. When you handle disagreements constructively, your entire family learns how to navigate challenging moments and emerge stronger. Instead of avoiding conflict at all costs, think of it as a valuable tool for growth, both for you and your children. Every argument or standoff presents an opportunity to teach problem-solving, patience, and negotiation. When handled with intention, these moments show your child how to express themselves honestly, listen to others, and find solutions rather than complain. You teach, by example, how to find the chance for growth in each challenge.

Tackling conflict begins with slowing down enough to recognize what's happening beneath the surface. Disagreements can look like arguments over bedtime, chores, or screen time. Yet the true root can be deeper. Maybe your child feels ignored when you're busy with work. Perhaps you're running on empty and have no patience left for messes in the living room.

Recognizing and naming the real issue is a vital step. This might mean pausing a heated discussion to say, "Let's figure out what's bothering us here." Often, simply naming the frustration can reduce its power. Once you identify the root cause, you can move closer to finding a genuine solution without assigning blame.

Turning a conflict into a learning experience is an engaging goal for the whole family. You'll be able to include your child in the process, regardless of their age. Even little ones can help brainstorm solutions if you frame the problem in a way that makes sense to them. "We keep fighting over toys. What ideas do you have so everyone gets a turn?" For older children or teens, ask them directly for their perspective. "What would make this fairer for everyone?"

Brainstorming together gives children a sense of ownership over the outcome. It teaches them that their ideas are valued and matter. It's helpful to write down all possible solutions together. No idea is too silly. Then talk through the pros and cons of each one. This step can transform a shouting match into an opportunity for teamwork.

Choosing a plan that meets as many needs as possible evolves from evaluating what each person wants. Some call this a compromise. It's not about one person giving in completely. It's about finding the sweet spot to create a mutually beneficial outcome. You may have to give up something small. Maybe bedtime is shifted by ten minutes, or screen time is earned by completing homework first. The key is showing your child that flexibility goes both ways and that you value their input.

Modeling calm reasoning encourages negotiation. "I know you want more time on your tablet, and I want to be sure you get enough sleep. What if we set a timer, and then read together for ten minutes before bed?" This is how children learn to find mutual wins—solutions where nobody feels like a loser.

Negotiating isn't about splitting things down the middle. It's about considering everyone's needs and feelings. This teaches your child how to stand up for themselves without steamrolling others, and also how to compromise without resentment.

These are skills that a child will use in friendships, school projects, and in future relationships. As your child sees you model negotiation — instead of demanding obedience or giving up in frustration —they learn how to cooperate with others without losing their voice.

What does this look like in everyday family life? Imagine siblings fighting over household chores. Instead of assigning jobs unilaterally or punishing them when things don't get done, you call a family meeting. Lay out the problem. "Chores aren't getting finished, and it's causing arguments." Ask each child how they feel about their current jobs, and what changes might help. Maybe one child hates vacuuming, yet doesn't mind dusting. Another child wants more help with trash duty. Together, you shuffle tasks until each child feels heard, even if nobody gets exactly what they want. This demonstrates to children how collective problem-solving works within your family team.

How do you apply these principles to other challenging issues? Identify the underlying problem behind a symptom, brainstorm potential solutions, negotiate a compromise that feels fair to all parties, and follow through as a cohesive team. Repeat this process each day for the next two months to form a new habit that you love, and your family will love the results.

Over time, these habits change how your whole family approaches disagreement. Instead of dreading conflict or avoiding tough conversations, everyone trusts there's a system for working things out fairly. Children grow up feeling confident in their ability to handle disagreements without shutting down or lashing out. They see firsthand that healthy resolutions come from communication and respect, not from shouting or silent treatment.

The beauty of conflict resolution is that it gives everyone a chance to practice skills they'll rely on for life, which include listening, speaking up, adapting, empathizing, and collaborating on shared goals.

Family life will never be argument-free. Yet every disagreement can be an invitation to build trust and resilience rather than resentment or distance. Teaching these skills by example means fewer blow-ups and more wins for your home team.

SET BOUNDARIES WITH CLEAR RULES FOR FAMILY HARMONY

Setting boundaries creates an invisible framework that holds a family together. When everyone knows what's expected, life at home becomes less chaotic and more predictable. Children, from toddlers to teens, crave structure even if they push against it. Predictability gives them a sense of security, helping them understand where freedom ends and respect for self and others begins. Boundaries aren't about control or constant correction. They're about building a safe environment where everyone feels valued and protected.

Setting effective boundaries starts with clarity. It's tempting to rattle off vague requests like, "Behave yourself," or "Don't make a mess." Yet these leave too much room for interpretation. A child needs specifics. "Shoes come off at the door." "Homework gets done before screen time." Using concrete, concise language leaves no doubt about what is expected. State the rule, and stick to it. Avoid setting too many boundaries at once, especially with little ones.

Enforcing boundaries is vital to protect your family's peace and safety. Consistency is the backbone of boundary enforcement. Following through on consequences every time, without favoritism or empty threats, teaches children that you mean what you say. If you announce that there will be no dessert after dinner if chores aren't done, you stick with it every time.

Inconsistency breeds anxiety and power struggles, while predictability builds trust. It's not always easy to implement, especially after a long day. Yet consistency pays off in fewer arguments down the road. If you slip up, acknowledge it to your children. "I blew it. Sorry about that." Then get back on track without guilt.

Communicating boundaries correctly makes all the difference in how they're received. Speak in a calm, firm tone, never harsh or shaming. Explain the reason behind the rule when possible. "We put away toys, so no one trips and gets hurt." "Phones off at dinner so we can enjoy each other's company." When children know why a rule exists, they're more likely to cooperate, even if they disagree. Involving older children in discussions about boundaries and consequences gives them a voice in family rules and promotes a willingness to respect them.

Do parents need boundaries, too? Boundaries work best when they apply to everyone. Children watch adults for cues on how seriously to take any rule. If the rule is "No yelling", yet you regularly lose your temper, the rule loses its power. When you establish clear expectations for everyone's behavior, grown-ups included, confusion fades and connection grows. (see APA list: 23)

How do you hold yourself to the standards you set for your children? Apologizing when you fall short shows them how to recover from missteps. This reveals your commitment to honoring healthy boundaries and enhancing family interactions as you lead by example.

How might boundaries change over time? Consider the classic rule: "No phones at the dinner table." At first, there might be eye-rolling or protests, especially from teens accustomed to scrolling through their feeds during meals. Over time, this boundary provides an opportunity for emotional bonding. Dinner becomes a time for honest conversations, shared stories, laughter, and even awkward silences that invite someone to speak up. A child sees that you are paying attention and that family time matters more than notifications.

Flexibility does have a place in boundary enforcement. As children grow up, some exceptions make sense. What if your college student can't be home for Sunday dinner but would like to join you? Here's how we handled that in my family. We placed a cell phone on the table at my college son's place. Via speaker phone, he could be part of our dinner conversation. This doesn't break a boundary. This act of love is an adaptation to maintain strong family ties.

Remember that boundaries aren't barriers, but bridges that bring everyone together in shared values and clear expectations. With a healthy structure in place, warmth, self-control, responsibility, and adaptability can grow.

Next, you will explore savvy ways to fit regular self-care into your busy life and the reasons to do so.

CHAPTER 7
SELF-CARE FOR STRESSED PARENTS

PRIORITIZE "ME TIME": THE ART OF SELF-CARE

YOU MIGHT RESIST the idea of "Me Time" when you're stressed by chasing a deadline and scraping dried oatmeal off the car seat. That's the time to embrace self-care, not resist it. Why?

You embrace self-care because parenting without it is a recipe for exhaustion. You know that feeling when your battery flashes red and every request for a snack, homework help, or another bedtime story sounds like fire alarms? That's your inner warning sign that something needs attention. Too often, parents push through, telling themselves there's no time for "Me time". The truth is, neglecting your own needs doesn't make you a better parent. It drains your reserves, increases irritability, and turns even the most minor tasks into mountains.

Claiming personal time isn't selfish. It's an act of survival and love. When you carve out moments for yourself, you're not escaping your family. You're making sure you have something left to give them.

Emotional energy, much like a bank account, can't be spent endlessly without making deposits. Regular "Me Time" helps recharge your energy, refuel your patience, and reset your nervous system before burnout strikes.

You're not meant to operate on empty. When you pause to do something that brings joyful peace, you send a powerful message to your children: Their happiness matters, just as yours does. This balance helps prevent resentment. It keeps you grounded and energized, allowing you to be the kind of parent (and partner) you genuinely want to be.

The goal is to find time to recharge in a full schedule. Sometimes, it means listing "Me Time" on the family calendar, just as you would list soccer practice and work meetings. Suppose you treat personal time as a non-negotiable event. In that case, you're more likely to honor it and less likely to cancel when things get hectic.

Boundaries are your best friend here. Let your family know that when the door is closed or your favorite mug is out, that's a signal you're in "Me Time." Even ten minutes of quiet may renew you. If guilt creeps in, remember that everyone benefits when you return refreshed, rather than frazzled.

What do you do in your "Me Time"? That matters less than the fact that you're doing it. Choose activities that fill your creative well and spark a sense of lightness. Curl up with a book that makes you lose track of time. Pick up that instrument gathering dust, and play it. Blast an upbeat song and dance, earning bonus points if this reminds you of carefree times before becoming a parent. Sink your hands into dirt and plant flowers that will lure butterflies and hummingbirds to your window all summer long. Book a massage to let someone else knead away tension, while you drift into bliss. Channel your inner Jackson Pollock, painting a canvas in time to a favorite tune.

What do you do with an old habit that no longer serves you, like late-night snacking, doom-scrolling, or collapsing in front of the TV? You might replace it with something you love that loves you back. Two months of repeating a new activity each day can form a new habit you love, which loves you back by helping you thrive.

When self-care becomes a routine rather than a rare occurrence, your parenting style shifts. You find more patience when little hands make a mess. You pause before snapping at a partner for forgetting to stop at the cleaners. Emotional regulation becomes easier, even automatic, when you're no longer running on fumes. Regular self-care also fills in what you feel is lacking, such as confidence, creativity, and even a desire for connection or romance. You start to feel whole again, not just the manager of everyone else's needs.

There's something almost magical about moving your body to sweat out frustration, like doing hot yoga under the sun or dancing until the stars blur into dreamtime. Stored toxins and negative energy depart in every drop of sweat, replaced by optimism and resilience that lasts longer than any spa day. As you fulfill yourself by doing more of what you love, you revive energy for more laughter, hugs, deep talks, and even happy, sexy love with your beloved.

SELECT YOUR SELF-CARE MENU & REFLECTION EXERCISE

Create Your Self-Care Menu: List ten activities that lift your mood or help you unwind. Post this list near your toothbrush. While you brush, select a favorite activity and schedule "Me time" to complete it.

Reflection Prompts: After each self-care session, note the status of your PIES: Your Physical, Intellectual, Emotional, and Spiritual health. Notice shifts in parenting and partnering that day.

MAKE YOUR MIND SUPPORT SELF-CARE BY ASKING A DAILY QUESTION

It's estimated that over half of our daily behaviors, decisions, and even many biological processes are driven by the subconscious mind, according to research and sources like **James Clear (Atomic Habits), Bruce Lipton (The Biology Of Belief), Dr. Joe Dispenza (Becoming Supernatural), and Gerald Zaltman, a Harvard Business School Professor.**

Suppose you hold a subconscious belief like, "I never have any time for myself." Your subconscious mind will release that false belief and accept a new, true one that you impress on it through daily repetition and elevated emotion. You'll reap the benefits of the new belief, like making time for self-care.

Is it best to give your subconscious mind a command to support self-care or ask it a question? Your mind could get stuck on a command like, "Show me how to fit self-care into my day." It's best to ask a "How" question, which invites your brain to shift into an active, problem-solving state and generate ideas, leading to more effective and creative solutions. How do you frame your best question?

Inspire your subconscious mind to support self-care by asking a daily "How" question that you frame in five steps:

1. Set a goal to pursue each day for the next two months to make it a new habit. Since we're focusing on self-care, your goal may be, "I will find 10 to 20 minutes for my self-care today."
2. Turn your goal into a HOW question. Your mind loves searching for answers to a clearly stated question, such as, "How do I find 20 minutes to love myself with self-care today?" Or, "How do I find 20 minutes to fit self-care into my busy day?"
3. Ask yourself that question out loud or write it down every day for at least 60 consecutive days. This is the minimum amount of time it takes to form a new habit you love that loves you back by producing feel-good brain chemicals.
4. Look for evidence that answers your daily question. Listen for a whisper of intuition. Notice opportunities to squeeze in some self-care. Take action on coincidences or cancelled appointments that open a window for "Me Time."
5. Continue to ask your daily question, "How do I find 20 minutes to love myself with self-care today?" Embrace the answers and synchronicities that arise when you treat yourself to 10 to 20 delightful minutes of self-care.

Do you see how carving out "Me Time" can help nurture the strongest, happiest version of yourself? When you consistently show up for yourself, you'll quickly see how everyone benefits.

REDUCE STRESS TECHNIQUES FOR QUICK RELIEF ON BUSY DAYS

You know those days when your heart feels like it's racing a marathon and your mind is juggling a dozen tabs at once? Maybe you're running late, your phone won't stop buzzing, and the dog just tracked mud across your bedsheets. Stress becomes a background hum that's hard to silence. Fortunately, you don't need an hour or a fancy retreat to reset your nerves. Sometimes, even a few minutes can make a difference.

What's the quickest stress relief? Remember, it often starts with your breath. Each deep breath serves as a reset button, telling your brain that all is well and asking your fight-or-flight amygdala to calm down, so you can fully enjoy the moment.

What if your mind is spinning too fast to focus on breathing? Guided visualization may be your shortcut to serenity. A favorite tool like Brain Tap offers 10- or 20-minute audio sessions that combine calming voice prompts with gentle pulses of light and sound. It feels like a mini-vacation for your brain. Pop on the headset, and let someone guide you into a brain fitness spa, emerging on the other side more refreshed. One session can restore patience, refresh inspiration, and maximize productivity for the rest of the day. Doing a "yoga nidra" produces a similar effect, without having to buy special equipment.

Sometimes the best way to manage stress is to take quick breaks rather than pushing through. Research shows that even a 10 or 20-minute nap can reboot your motivation, much like it did for Einstein. He'd hold a marble egg while he drifted into nap time. When the egg he was holding fell onto the floor, it woke him. A quick nap shifted his brain waves from stressed to refreshed.

Since it worked for Einstein, I wanted to see how it works for me. After a brief nap, I find myself thinking more clearly and moving through tasks with greater ease. These micro-breaks aren't wasted time. They're investments in greater productivity and steadier moods. If a nap isn't possible, then step outside for fresh air and stretching. A shift in scenery can work wonders.

What do you do when time is tight and frustration is rising?

MOVE FROM FRUSTRATED TO FULFILLED EXERCISE

Redirect your thoughts from what's frustrating to what's working. **Why bother?** Because feeling frustrated, irritated, or overwhelmed can open the gates to complaints, which are linked to health risks.

Science says that even a single minute of complaining can physically alter your brain, flooding your system with stress hormones, weakening memory circuits, and reprogramming your mind to expect threats, even in safe circumstances. That's how frustration-triggered complaints can turn seemingly harmless words into structural changes in the brain. (see APA list: 77, 78, 79, 80)

The Good News: You can rewire your brain in the opposite state with techniques such as shifting perspectives and expressing gratitude for what's working, as you will do now.

SHIFT PERSPECTIVE WITH A MIRROR EXERCISE

Stand in front of the mirror. Look yourself in the eyes. Name the three best things you did today. Thank yourself for creating these wins. What you say to yourself can change the trajectory of your life, so speak to yourself as if you were your best friend.

Building quick-fix strategies into a busy day develops a habit of replacing moments of tension with moments of relief. Remember, science says that daily practice makes permanent.

CREATE YOUR STRESS-BUSTER CHECKLIST

Keep this handy checklist somewhere you'll see it daily, on your fridge or as a phone note. When stress spikes, select one or two techniques to restore calm:

- Box breathing for one minute. 20-second inhale through your nose. 20-second hold. 20-second exhale with a long sigh. Repeat until your heart rate calms.
- Guided visualization (Brain Tap or app)
- Power nap (10–20 minutes)
- Rock out with a favorite song
- Gratitude journaling (three entries)
- Mirror pep talk: three wins today
- Ask A Daily Question: How do I find 20 minutes to love myself with self-care?

Try mixing and matching self-care activities throughout the week until you find your personal favorites—notice which ones help you feel calm, even in the midst of chaos.

PLAN PARENTAL TRADITIONS FOR SELF-CARE

Tending to your relationship is an emotionally intelligent choice for healthy self-care, since happy relationships are a key to extending your happy longevity, according to a **30-year-long Harvard study of married couples** and a **20-year study by psychologist John Gottman.**

I encourage parents to plan a weekly date night tradition when you focus on each other, rather than your children, duties, or deadlines. Date night is your time to uncover something new about each other and be playful, enjoying healthy doses of adult fun and laughter that spark happy, sexy love that lasts.

BUILD A SUPPORT NETWORK: YOU'RE NOT ALONE

Parenting in isolation can feel like you're hiking up a mountain, pushing a boulder that nobody else sees. The hardest part may be feeling like you're the only one struggling. Creating a strong support network changes that. It gives you relief, a place to vent without judgment, and reassurance that what you're feeling is both normal and surmountable. When frustration builds, talking with another parent who's been there may lift your mood in a single conversation. The presence of a like-minded adult who listens, brings peace to your panic, or nods in understanding, can make your day.

How do you find a connection that heals what ails you? Events at your child's school or places of worship may open doors to connection. Volunteering for field trips, joining the PTA, or even chatting with other parents in the pick-up line can create bonds that deepen over time. Faith communities often have built-in support through shared values and traditions. Attending services, small group discussions, or family nights introduces you to others who know the joys and the sheer exhaustion of raising children. Exploring common bonds with neighbors through community events, such as block parties, book clubs, and neighborhood clean-ups, helps you meet people who might become trusted confidants.

What if you're juggling work shifts with little flexibility to leave home? Online forums can replace in-person meetings. Websites and social media groups dedicated to parenting offer advice, solidarity, and a place to vent or celebrate, anonymously if desired. You'll find specialized spaces for single parents, parents of a child with special needs, blended families, and more. These online communities unite people who "get it" and won't minimize your concerns.

Parenting workshops and seminars, sometimes hosted by local therapists or schools, also bring parents together to share stories and set common goals to pursue in a supportive, safe environment.

You can track progress toward common community goals using the Streaks app and the Strava Social app.

For single parents navigating solo, support networks are even more critical. Parenting alone multiplies stress and decision fatigue. Finding others in similar situations alleviates a sense of isolation and provides mutual support.

The beauty of support networks is that you show up as you are — a perfectly imperfect person, who may be tired out yet hopeful.. A shared laugh during volunteer night may be the start of a new friendship with a like-minded parent.

BALANCE WORK AND FAMILY LIFE TECHNIQUES: FINDING YOUR RHYTHM

Is there any parent who feels no stress from juggling work demands and family life? Maybe you rush to get dinner on the table after a long day, yet your mind's still stuck on issues at the office. The constant pull of due dates and family time feels like your feet are in two adjacent canoes. Move forward? You're sunk. Competing priorities creep into every hour. There's the pressure of answering late-night texts from work, and guilt for missing your child's hockey goal, because you were on a Zoom meeting. Weekends vanish in a blur as you try to make up for missed moments and check off your family to-do list.

Finding any balance in this swirl is tough, yet it isn't impossible. The key is drawing clear lines between work and home, even if both happen in the same room. You make family time a priority by scheduling it, like a client meeting, and "Me time". Block off Friday pizza night or Saturday family walks. Protect those windows fiercely. Parents have revived depleted energy by treating weekends as sacred: No work emails. No sneaking off to finish a report.

Children know when you're fully present. So does your stress level. Sometimes the lines blur. That's real life. Still, prioritizing clear work-family boundaries helps you regain a sense of control in your week. (see APA List: 69)

Time management may feel like a game you can't win, yet the Pareto Principle (the 80/20 rule) flips the script. This principle suggests that

80% of results come from just 20% of your efforts. In other words, not every task deserves equal attention. Identify the handful of activities, both at work and at home, that make a significant impact. Perhaps it's prepping meals on Sunday so you're not scrambling each evening, or focusing on key projects instead of responding to every email instantly. Once you identify the high-impact tasks, prioritize them at the forefront of your schedule for both work and family life. (see APA list: 27)

Dedicate most of your energy to these critical few. Then delegate or drop the rest where possible. Consider automating repetitive chores. Set up bill pay online, use grocery delivery services, and teach older children how to tackle laundry and make healthy snacks.

Time-blocking can save the day. Set aside specific time slots for work calls, chores, homework help, and family meals. One mom adds color codes to her calendar, so everyone knows when she's working, when she's available for play, and when she expects quiet for her tasks. She even taught her middle schooler how to use this system for homework, chores, and free time.

Tools like the free and paid versions of the Eisenhower Matrix Google Sheet Templates can help you prioritize tasks by importance and urgency into quadrants such as "Do now," "Delegate," "Schedule," and "Delete."

Please don't get drawn into handling only emergencies while neglecting meaningful moments. Review your efforts every week and adjust as needed. Flexibility matters more than sticking to a perfect plan.

Focusing on what matters most, rather than saying "Yes" to everything, lightens busy days. You have more energy for bedtime stories or backyard races when you're not bogged down with endless tiny tasks. What changes in families who embrace time management at home? A significant change may be the sigh of relief that comes when everyone sits together, without screens or rush. That priceless presence is worth preserving.

REDUCE STRESS WITH MINDFUL PARENTING

When it comes to parenting, life rarely follows a script. As you face each stressor, you improvise. You might answer emails with one hand, flip pancakes with the other, and half-listen as your child tells you about their latest dream. Multitasking feels like the new normal, yet dividing focus makes it impossible to look beneath the surface to find deeper meanings. Do you know what a better alternative is?

Mindful parenting is about shifting gears. It's choosing to show up fully present with your child. It's noticing when you're on autopilot, catching yourself before a reflexive snap, consciously responding to what's happening beneath the surface, and finding the subtext of what's being said.

One of the greatest gifts you give your child is your attention. When you practice mindful parenting, you reduce the number of automatic, knee-jerk reactions that often arise when stress is high and patience is low.

What if you're about to tune out what's being asked of you? Instead, you pause and imagine being in your child's shoes.

Maybe you remember to ask a favorite question. "Do you want me to hear you, help you, or hug you?" Giving your whole-hearted response gives your child a healthy dose of your undivided attention. Being present can become a loving habit that consistently leads to mutually beneficial outcomes.

Incorporating mindfulness into daily family life isn't as complicated as it may sound. Mindful listening is like active listening. When your child speaks, look them in the eye, set aside distractions, and tune in, not just to their words, but also to their mood and body language.

You can also bring mindfulness into family routines by enjoying quick rituals together. A favorite ritual of my young children was improvising stories before they went to bed. At one stage, Captain Hook usually showed up on his ship for adventures on the creek by our house. We experienced how mindful play can replace stress with creative fun in a memorable bedtime routine.

Nurturing creativity opens a doorway to mindfulness and playful connection for both parents and children. Put on a favorite soundtrack and paint a canvas together in rhythm to the music. Or hand out pots and pans, and then clang your "instruments" as you march together. Memories of your shared creative adventures may fill your heart with joy whenever you recall them, long after your children are happily launched into the world.

The impact of mindful parenting ripples through every relationship in your home. When you slow down and offer undivided attention, you limit misunderstandings and deepen interactions. You become more attuned to what's going on beneath your child's words. You sense if they're scared about a new school, or just craving closeness after a long day apart. Empathy comes easier when you're calmly present. You pick up on cues that would otherwise fly under the radar. You respond with compassion instead of frustration.

Children also learn mindfulness by example. When they see you regulating your reactions and listening with patience, they know how to do the same with siblings, friends, and even teachers. Mindfulness gives a child skills for life: How to calm themselves when upset, how to focus when distracted, and how to notice their feelings without being ruled by them. For families who face frequent conflicts and intense emotions, these skills can be transformative.

MAKE MINDFULNESS REAL WITH YOUR CHILD IN A DAILY EXERCISE

Maybe it's three minutes of quiet breathing together before dinner or sharing one thing you noticed that day while walking outside. Notice what changes —not just in your child, but in yourself. If it feels odd at first, that's okay. Every new habit begins awkwardly until it becomes a permanent part of your routine through daily practice.

Remember that mindful parenting is less about chasing calm and more about showing up with open eyes, ears, and an open heart. Presence is the thread that weaves together a loving family tapestry of stronger bonds and greater resilience, even when family life is unpredictable.

Next, you'll see how to stay calm in the face of everyday parenting stressors.

CHAPTER 8
REAL-LIFE PARENTING SCENARIOS

BE CALM IN THE CHAOS OF THE MORNING RUSH

SUPPOSE you're in the kitchen, scrambling eggs without burning them. At the same time, you help one child button a school shirt and another child pick up a homework assignment from the floor. The morning rush can feel like a relay race, where the baton gets dropped and nobody wins. Being calm in chaos is a learned skill that helps you show up without losing your cool.

Morning stressors are universal for parents. Getting children out of bed can be a struggle that feels personal. Yet often it's simply biology. A child's natural sleep cycle rarely aligns with schools' early start times.

How do you reduce morning chaos? One strategy is to set up your morning environment the night before. Pick out clothes and lay them out, including socks and shoes. This five-minute investment pays off daily. Make sure that backpacks contain completed homework. Double-check for forms and library books. Fill lunchboxes and prepare as much of breakfast as possible ahead of time.

Nightly prep rituals can turn morning mad dashes into cozy send-offs. Setting a positive tone first thing in the morning can significantly impact everyone's day.

Start by using an alarm that wakes you with gentle tones instead of a nerve-wracking noise. Instead of barking frantic orders, greet your child warmly, even if you're both still waking up.

Try keeping breakfast phone-free, so everyone has a chance to connect without notifications or emails pulling you away from your family time. This is sacred time, even if it's just ten minutes over cereal. You create a buffer against stress throughout the day with positive morning rituals, such as sharing what you're looking forward to or telling a silly joke.

LIFT MOODS AND ENERGIZE BRAINS WITH BREAKFAST HARMONIZING

Music is a key that opens a closed heart, gives wings to the mind, and flight to the imagination. When words fail, music speaks. Plato's insights reveal how music empowers you and your family to make it a great day.

Listening to a favorite song, even while eating breakfast, engages nearly the whole brain, producing feel-good brain chemicals, reducing stress hormones, and increasing vagal tone. It's not magic. It's neuro-chemical regulation as the brain uses the sound of music to release a chemical cocktail of reward, regulation, and connection. (see APA list: 60, 61)

Singing a favorite song together as a family also boosts oxytocin, the bonding love hormone. That's why singing lullabies bonds the singer with the child, and why group singing in a choir or a band builds social connections. (see APA list: 92) Is there a favorite family song you might sing to start the day with a dose of bonding love?

Moving to music revs up enthusiasm for possibilities. Remember the ROCKY theme song? Could you choose a family theme song that energizes your inner champions and launches an excellent day for each of you? Have some fun listening to theme songs that you and your family suggest. Select the song that gives you chills or gets you moving with a musical dose of feel-good neurochemical brain fuel to launch your day.

Field unexpected curve balls in the morning rush. No matter how well you plan, mornings still can throw curveballs like an unexpected tantrum, or suddenly realizing gym shoes are still in yesterday's mud puddle.

Remember: Staying calm in stress is emotionally contagious, showing your child how to face unforeseen challenges with peace, not panic.

What if something goes off track? Pause and take a deep breath—out loud and on purpose. Narrate what you're doing. "I'm taking a breath before I figure out what to do next." Explaining this helps with real-time emotional regulation. It shows a child that unexpected frustration is familiar, yet it doesn't have to darken your day (see APA list, source 3).

REFLECT ON THE MORNING RUSH EXERCISE

Take a moment after drop-off or before work to jot down three things that went well this morning, even if they're tiny wins like everyone finding their shoes or sharing a smile at breakfast. Next, write one thing you'd like to improve tomorrow. Over the week, you'll spot patterns. What steps always trip you up? Does upbeat music smooth out rough starts? Celebrate even baby-step improvements. Progress promotes progress.

Be empowered by knowing that the tone you set in these first moments together lingers long after everyone has parted ways for the day. When you approach the morning rush with intention, helpful rituals, and flexibility, you're not just moving bodies out the door. You're nourishing loved ones. You're nurturing connection and calm that carries into every part of everyone's day.

NAVIGATE ACADEMIC STRESS AND HOMEWORK HASSLES: TOOLS AND TECHNIQUES

Procrastination is a regular visitor in many homes, as children of all ages find creative ways to delay doing their homework. Parents might help a child identify a reason for the delay. Does an assignment feel like a mountain they can't climb? Do you happen to know if the directions are clear? Is a workspace cluttered with old mail, noisy siblings, or a flickering TV that distracts focus?

Setting up a dedicated workspace and allocating a regular time each day for homework can provide comfort and predictability in school day routines. Select a quiet corner or a small desk, away from distractions such as screens and toys. Stock it with school supplies. Provide a nourishing after-school snack. Set a timer for 20-30 minutes of focused work, followed by a five-minute break to stretch, snack, and move around. This structure of regular breaks helps your child stay on track and be less likely to spiral into stress.

Your encouragement can be a powerful antidote to homework delays. Please feel free to comment on the effort your child put in. Mentioning progress builds confidence and motivation. "I saw you get started right away today." Or, "You kept trying even when it got tricky." Avoid hovering or jumping in with criticism if your child doesn't "get it" quickly. Instead, be a quiet presence. Perhaps you ask to sit nearby while you do your work, showing support without stifling independence.

Conflicts over homework are almost inevitable. Tensions rise and tired brains clash when patience thins. Instead of snapping or issuing ultimatums, you may shift into problem-solving mode together. If your child says math is hard or grammar is confusing, first acknowledge their feelings. "It sounds like this is tough tonight." Then, determine what is blocking them by asking open-ended questions. "What part feels hardest?" "What do you think will help?"

Strive to collaborate on solutions. Does the assignment need to be broken into small steps? Can a different explanation be found in a video or online resource to clear up confusion?

What if you find yourself stumped by advanced material that looks nothing like the homework you did at their age? You can admit this truth. "Wow, this is tricky. I'm learning right beside you." You model resourcefulness by looking up answers together.

Let go of the pressure to have all the answers. You can teach your child, by example, to seek help and persist through challenges. Discussing difficulties makes it safe for a child to admit when they're stuck, instead of pretending all is well or shutting down. Encourage your child to self-advocate by writing questions for their teacher or by brainstorming what kind of help would clear up any confusion. Making this a daily habit builds self-confidence.

Let's review how to avoid homework minefields: Be proactive. Set up a supportive environment. Comment on moments of effort. Explore solutions together, reducing frustration.

This approach teaches your child more than algebra or spelling. They learn that asking for help is a strength, enabling the work to be done and developing problem-solving skills.

ENSURE HOMEWORK SUCCESS CHECKLIST

Create a simple checklist with your child:

- Is my workspace ready?
- Do I have all my supplies?
- Do I take regular breaks to move around?
- Do I ask for help when I need it?
- Do I notice when I did something well today?

Review it together each week and celebrate improvements, no matter how minor. This turns a dreaded homework battle into a chance for teamwork.

MEDIATE SIBLING RIVALRY WITHOUT A REFEREE WHISTLE OR A LECTURE

Sibling rivalry often emerges over minor injustices, fueled by something real beneath the surface. Children have a radar that tracks equal treatment from their parents. Arguing over who gets to ride shotgun is a fight for more of your time and attention. Be considerate of each child's need for you to see, hear, and value them equally. When one child feels that another is getting more of your attention, the jealous monster arises to argue its case.

When inevitable conflicts arise, it's tempting to lay down the law. Yet mediation works better than referee whistles or lectures.

Start with a pause before reactions escalate. Bring the children together and ask them to share their perspectives on what happened. No blaming. No interrupting. Each sibling takes a turn. For younger children, it helps to have them use simple "I feel" statements. "I feel mad because she took my marker." With older children, encourage more detailed responses. Your goal is to keep the conversation on track as they name emotions, without blame. If tempers are high, I would suggest that each of you take a few deep breaths to lower the heat.

Facilitating these discussions means guiding siblings toward their solutions, rather than announcing verdicts. Ask open-ended questions, like "What would help each of you feel better about this?" And encourage them to brainstorm ideas together. "Is there a way you can take turns?" If their ideas are silly or impractical, say, "There are no bad ideas." This process calms a storm and provides tools to resolve conflicts independently. You're ending an argument and raising future adults who can find mutually-agreeable solutions.

Cooperation doesn't happen by accident. It's built over time with practice and encouragement. Family projects and shared chores are excellent ways to foster teamwork and collaboration. One summer, I initiated a home care boot camp so that my children would learn how to bathe the dog, make dinner, do the dishes together, do their laundry, and clean their rooms. You can still catch teens being good by acknowledging times when they work together as a team and when they meet or exceed expectations on home-care routines.

You can reduce sibling rivalry even in young children by creating transparent and fair rules that everyone understands. No favorites. No secret exceptions.

Lay out expectations for activities such as taking turns with toys, selecting TV shows, and dividing household chores. Post these agreements where all can see them. Seeing it written down may stop an argument before it starts. Enforce consequences consistently.

Please ensure the rules are flexible enough to accommodate a child's evolving needs and abilities. If one child feels another child always gets special treatment, resentment builds. If you check in often, a child will tell you if a change is needed.

BUILD ONE HABIT THAT CHANGES THE WHOLE FAMILY DYNAMIC

Teach your child to accept full responsibility for their own choices, actions, and results, as you do now.

How do you teach this? You teach by example when you model this behavior. If you start yelling or react out of frustration, take full responsibility. "I yelled at you because I was upset about something else. I'm sorry." This shows children that we can all make regrettable choices and that we have the power to make things right.

LET SIBLING RIVALRY BE A PART OF FAMILY LIFE WITHOUT CONSTANT CONFLICTS

When you address the root causes of a conflict —such as vying for attention and arguing for fairness —you create space for genuine connection.

When you teach children skills of mediation, cooperation, and responsibility, you reduce rivalries and enrich the family dynamic.

When each person feels valued and accountable, space opens up for understanding and bonding between siblings who were once locked in battles.

MANAGE ANGER IN STRESSFUL PUBLIC MELTDOWNS

Few parenting tests are as nerve-wracking as a public meltdown. You're walking your young child to the airplane restroom when they suddenly drop to the floor, wailing, kicking, or flat-out refusing to budge. Heads turn. You can feel eyes on you. Some sympathetic. Some not so much. You might feel your cheeks burning as a wave of embarrassment, helplessness, or anger washes over you. You think that people are grading your parenting in real time.

In these moments, the goal is to calm yourself first, before your child. The pressure to keep your composure skyrockets when you're in public. Children sense your tension. Their distress feeds off yours, creating a feedback loop that can escalate fast. Instead of matching their volume or snapping back, try lowering your voice. Speak softly, almost in a whisper. This unexpected calm draws your child's attention and can slow the emotional storm. Try kneeling to eye level, gently saying, "I know you're upset. I'm here with you." Even if you feel shaky, projecting steadiness helps calm you and your child.

Redirecting focus is a powerful tool in high-pressure moments. There's no point in trying to reason with a child who is in a state of panic. Instead, you might distract them by gently touching their shoulder and asking for their help in finding something. Distracting a child can help them disengage from a spiral of distress.

Planning goes a long way in lowering the risk of public outbursts. When planning outings, think like a scout. Anticipate what might spark trouble and pack accordingly. Hungry kids have short tempers, so stash healthy snacks in your bag for quick energy. A bored child often finds their entertainment (not always to your liking), so consider bringing small toys or books for waiting rooms and long lines. A sleep-deprived child can't cope well with stressors, so plan errand runs when a child is well-rested. What if certain places, like crowded malls and loud restaurants, are more likely to trigger a meltdown? Preparation can help prevent outbursts if you guide a child's expectations before you leave home. "We'll have ten minutes at the store, then we'll choose your snack for the ride home."

Even the best planning can't prevent every explosion. That's why it's helpful to reflect after the fact, not to beat yourself up, but to get smarter for next time. In a calm moment at home, sit with your child and talk about what happened in the meltdown. It's best to keep it simple and judgment-free. "You got upset at the store earlier. Tell me what made it so hard."

Listen for clues about triggers, such as a skipped nap, an overwhelming crowd, or feeling too hot or too cold. Then brainstorm together. "What could we do next time if you start to feel that way?" You might ask your child to help you pack a play kit next time.

This reflection isn't just for your child. It helps you as well. Notice which emotions their meltdown stirred in you. Was it an embarrassment? Anger? Did you feel powerless or judged? Write down what helped you stay calm (or what didn't). Consider making adjustments for future excursions, such as deciding to leave the store in a meltdown or heading out after lunch next time.

REFLECT ON A MELTDOWN EXERCISE

After a public meltdown, take five minutes once home to reflect on what happened in your **Manage Anger With Love Journal.** Jot down:

- What triggered the outburst?
- How did I react in the moment?
- What helped de-escalate (if anything)?
- How did my child recover afterward?
- What's one thing I can do differently next time?

You'll start to notice patterns, such as specific times of day, particular stores, or even certain foods that trigger them. Over time, this practice builds insight. You'll feel more confident in handling public outbursts and have less concern over what others think. The goal is to learn together, and show your child that your loving support doesn't depend on their stellar behavior in aisle nine.

REDUCE TECHNOLOGY TENSIONS TO RESTORE CALM

Disagreements about limiting screen time may breed resentment in a child and increase your anxiety about their exposure to risky online content.

Teens seek privacy, yet the vastness of the internet means they might see things they're not ready for. Even young children can stumble onto unsafe content. The push-pull between freedom and safety can anger both sides.

You may ease this friction by developing a family media plan that sets clear, consistent technology boundaries. This plan works best when it's based on a collaborative discussion and a written agreement, rather than a list of commands. Decide together which devices and apps are acceptable, how much screen time is allowed on school nights versus weekends, and where devices should be stored at night. A phone-free bedroom helps everyone sleep better. Also, your plan sets "screen-free" time, such as during meals or family outings. Keeping the plan visible and referring to it as necessary ensures everyone is on the same page.

For young children, maintaining parental access to emails and search histories is not considered spying. It's protecting a child until they're ready for more independence.

Experts now advise parents to keep active passwords for devices used by older children, and to regularly check their devices to identify potential online threats and scams targeting children of all ages.

To keep your teen safe while using ChatGPT, it's also wise to activate parental controls, a feature that debuted in October 2025.

Specific time limits reduce the need for endless negotiations. For instance, "Thirty minutes of gaming after homework" is much clearer than saying, "Not too much." Tools like timers and built-in parental controls can enforce limits, so you're not always the bad guy. When children push back, as they often will, you frame the rules as a matter of health and safety, not punishment. Acknowledge your challenges, too. "Sometimes I scroll too long, so let's both work on this."

FRAME BOUNDARIES CORRECTLY TO PROMOTE COOPERATION

You can keep tech boundary communication open by describing boundaries as family care and by regularly asking what's working and what needs adjustment. Then you can adjust your media plan as required.

Ask your child what they like online, whether it's games, animal videos, or chatting with friends. Approach their experiences with curiosity, not criticism, so they'll come to you if something feels off. Discuss safety, bullying, and any unusual things a child mentions to keep the dialogue open.

Your actions matter more than your words. Children notice if you break the rules you set. If you check your phone at dinner or send work emails during family time, it signals that boundaries are flexible. You model healthy screen habits by setting your device aside and explaining why. "I'm putting this away so that I can focus on you." Make phone-free moments a shared activity, like placing devices in a basket during game night. Younger children especially learn by example. Even teens absorb these lessons, eye rolls aside.

When conflicts do arise, aim to remain calm and consistent, rather than escalating the situation. If a rule is broken, enforce the agreed-upon consequence without lecturing or shaming a child. "Our rule is no tablet after bedtime. Since it wasn't followed, we'll try again tomorrow."

CREATE YOUR FAMILY MEDIA AGREEMENT

Create your family media agreement together. Include curfews, screen-free areas, approved apps, and clear consequences for breaking rules. Hang it where everyone can see. Revisit it monthly and make adjustments as needed.

Technology will always be part of life. Similarly, there is a need for connection and trust within your home. How you handle tech tensions teaches your child more than any device ever could. With clear boundaries, open communication, and your good modeling, your family can manage technology and deepen connections.

Remember: Setting tech boundaries signals care. Balanced rules mean calmer days and stronger relationships, as screens become tools rather than minefields.

Have you ever wanted to break old patterns from your childhood upbringing? You'll discover how that works in the next chapter.

CHAPTER 9
BREAK INTERGENERATIONAL CYCLES AND MOVE PAST YOUR PAST

UNCOVER CHILDHOOD PATTERNS THAT IMPACT YOUR PARENTING TRIGGERS

SOME MOMENTS with your child jolt you, like seeing them tense after you raise your voice, or catching yourself using a phrase straight from your childhood, despite vowing never to repeat it. Your guilt afterward isn't all about what just happened. It's a sign that your upbringing is influencing your parenting.

Many parents' approach to raising children is shaped, for better or worse, by how they were raised. The way our parents handled discipline —whether they discussed emotions or not —and the way they showed affection leave lasting marks that can guide or hinder us, especially during times of stress.

I told you my story of how one parent's angry outbursts and use of physical punishment made me vow to do the opposite with my children, using the positive parenting strategies I've shared with you here. What's your story?

When you reflect on your childhood, specific patterns will emerge. What if your parents were quick-tempered, and now, under pressure, you too become harsh? What if emotions weren't discussed in your childhood, so expressing emotions with your child feels foreign to you? What if your school used physical punishment to maintain order? Discipline styles from your past —such as groundings, the silent treatment, and possibly corporal punishment —may be your default, even if you vowed to parent differently.

How your parents handled stress also affects you. If your mom yelled when overwhelmed and your dad retreated into silence, you may find yourself mimicking their reactions now. You may raise your voice or clam up before you realize it. These aren't flaws, but learned behaviors that can be changed.

SHINE A LIGHT ON YOUR CHILDHOOD PATTERNS EXERCISES

Self-reflection through in-depth journaling can help you see how your past influences your parenting as you explore these topics in your Journal:

Jot down ordinary childhood memories of how adults responded when you failed, expressed feelings, or needed love.

What did love look like in your house? Hugs and praise? Quieter gestures like packed lunches? Write without judgment. Look for repeating patterns. How did you react to a parent's angry outbursts? This can reveal old scripts that trigger your autopilot parenting today. Once you identify it, you can change it.

Track conflicts with your child and compare them to your own childhood experiences. Notice which situations trigger you. Is it bedtime fights, backtalk, or a constant state of chaos? After each tough moment, ask, "How does this remind me of my childhood?" Connections might be obvious. They may come through a sense of déjà vu or an outsized sense of frustration. If you ever think, "I sound just like my mother," pay attention to that clue.

By linking your current struggles to your past upbringing, you can free yourself from its grip.

Note instances of unconscious mimicry. We revert to phrases, rules, and reactions learned in childhood, especially under stress. If you were frequently criticized as a child, you may expect perfection from yourself or your child. You may snap at minor mishaps from old tensions, not a lack of love.

Note instances when you feel "not good enough." This may be an unresolved childhood wound that tends to resurface in parenting. Nagging feelings of inadequacy may amplify your distress or shame after a regrettable action.

Despite knowing that all parents slip up, your childhood wounds still can make minor setbacks feel like major flaws. How do you start recovering from those wounds?

Identify patterns to replace. When you feel triggered by a familiar irritant, pause and ask, 'Where have I felt this before?' What does it remind me of? When you name the feeling and its likely source, you unplug its power.

Note whether you feel self-compassion or lack it. Blaming yourself for old habits only deepens shame and delays change. Instead, treat yourself kindly. "I'm noticing old habits. This means I'm learning." By placing your hand over your heart as you breathe through difficult memories or challenging parenting moments, you can help regulate your emotions and signal safety that calms your nervous system.

REFLECT DEEPLY ON YOUR CHILDHOOD EXERCISE

Set aside 20 minutes to write or type three childhood memories involving discipline or strong emotion, positive or negative. For each memory, answer:

- How did I feel?
- What did I learn about myself or others?
- How do I see this memory show up in my parenting today?

When you finish, read it looking for repeating feelings or patterns. Are there reactions or phrases that you use with your children? End with a dose of self-kindness. "I give myself permission to grow beyond what I learned." Reflecting on your childhood may reveal why you feel stuck as an adult.

When you acknowledge these patterns without shame, you create space for new choices. This process can evoke emotions, such as sadness, anger, and even grief over what you missed out on. Feel it to free its grasp on you.

Your honest reflection is a decisive step toward breaking generational cycles. It's a courageous act of self-care for you now, and for the child you once were.

Every parent inherits some habits from their upbringing. Struggling to break from negative patterns is a sign of strength and resilience, not of failure. (see APA list: 28, 36)

CHANGE INTERGENERATIONAL PATTERNS NOW EXERCISE

As you strive for progress, guilt or shame may arise. Remind yourself that choosing change is an act of love for you, your children, and your partner or future partner. What worked for previous generations may not serve your best interests or your child's.

As you reflect, consider which values matter most to you as a parent. What legacy from your upbringing supports these values? What feels unhelpful or outdated? Decide what you want to keep and what to let go. (see APA list: 36)

This may mean setting new boundaries with relatives, who resist your changes. Let go of energy-draining habits and connect with energizing people, like you.

Greater self-awareness opens the door to more thoughtful parenting, even when stress or old triggers threaten to take over. (see APA list: 17, 28)

Each time you pause instead of reacting automatically, take a moment to celebrate your progress. Each time you choose empathy over impatience, celebrate your win to promote more wins.

What if old issues threaten to derail your parenting through self-doubt, harshness, or withdrawal? See them as signals where change is needed, not destiny.

You release old patterns when you choose new, healthier ways to respond in ways your brain accepts, rather than resists. Looking back kindly and honestly, you gain insights to improve your interactions today.

HEAL CHILDHOOD WOUNDS WITH SCIENCE-BACKED TOOLS AND TECHNIQUES

Healing past wounds with forgiveness and growth is a gift you give yourself, your children, and those who hurt you, even if they'll never know it.

Carrying old pain is exhausting. Resentment, anger, disappointment, and shame can linger in your body for years, subtly influencing everything from the way you react in stressful times to the warmth you're able to feel or offer to loved ones. Many parents wonder why they overreact to minor things or why specific memories trigger feelings of irritation or sadness. Their old injuries are still active beneath the surface.

Letting go of resentment toward childhood caregivers doesn't excuse what happened or diminish past harm. It simply acknowledges the need to move forward. This frees you from the tight grip of those memories, so you can start fresh. Sometimes, holding on to resentment feels safer because it offers a sense of control and an armor against threats. Over time, armor turns into a cage, which keeps you reacting out of pain rather than embracing joyful possibilities.

Acknowledging trauma is dealing honestly with past wounds. Suppose you grew up with criticism, neglect, chronic emotional distance, or excessive discipline. In each case, you may notice a rawness that flares up when your child says something hurtful or when your partner brings up an old wound.

It's empowering to say, "This happened to me. It hurt." That simple act can begin to loosen the grasp that your past has on your present.

When you embrace what you'd rather not face, you manage anger with love.

Naming the pain is the first step toward releasing it. Engaging in this work may evoke feelings of sadness, anger, and regret. These emotions ask you to focus on your unfulfilled needs. A common need is to practice forgiveness.

Forgiving doesn't mean you forget or deny what happened. Forgiveness asks you to stop carrying an emotional burden that someone else handed you. It may sound impossible to forgive at first, especially if the people who hurt you never apologized or admitted what they did. Yet forgiveness is something you do for yourself, not for them.

BEFRIEND A RADICAL HEALING TOOL EXERCISES

A robust method for this is "Radical Forgiveness," developed by Colin Tipping and outlined in *Radical Forgiveness: A Revolutionary Five-Stage Process to Heal Relationships, Let Go of Anger and Blame, and Find Peace in Any Situation.*

Radical forgiveness invites you to move through five stages: Telling your story. Feeling your feelings fully. Shifting your perspective. Releasing the energy of blame. Integrating new freedom into your life. Each stage peels back a layer of pain without denying the wound. (see APA list: 74)

What's the best time to utilize the radical forgiveness tool? The best time to forgive is NOW. I regret that I refused to forgive before the sudden death of my parent, who had the chronic habits of yelling and delivering harsh physical punishment to my brothers and me, the same way that this parent had been disciplined as a child.

I regret that I passed on the chance to release my childhood anger in a guided family therapy session that might have helped me feel closer to that parent before they died so young. Regret taught me a powerful lesson: If you don't forgive the parent or person who harmed you during their lifetime, it may take longer to reap the health benefits of forgiveness after their death. Yet it can be done by utilizing the tools, techniques, and exercises that you explore here.

Writing forgiveness letters, even though you don't send them, is a practical exercise. Forgiveness letters aren't sugar-coated. They are honest accounts of how someone's actions hurt you, and what you need to let go of now. Spend time describing how their behavior affected you as a child, and how it still echoes in your adult life. Then write what you wish they could have said or done differently. Finally, write how life would feel if you could release this pain. The act of writing helps organize lingering emotions, bringing clarity and relief, even if the person who hurt you is no longer alive or part of your life.

Feeling emotional release through guided visualizations is an effective technique. Close your eyes. Picture the person who hurt you, perhaps a parent, grandparent, or anyone who left painful marks. Visualize handing back the pain they gave you, and reclaiming your peace. It helps to imagine yourself as a child. Visualize your adult self giving you the loving kindness and protection that you lacked as a child.

Giving yourself what you feel is lacking effectively releases the feeling of lack.

Talking to a photo of the person who harmed you can take emotional weight off your shoulders. It frees you to release pent-up anger by describing how much pain they caused you and by telling them what you wanted and needed from them to help you feel safe and loved.

Keeping a "forgiveness journal" is a favorite tool. Use this space to note the hurts you're ready to release, and the new beliefs you want to nurture instead. Include statements such as, "I am worthy of kindness." "I can choose a new response." "I'm blessed to be a loving parent to my child and my younger self."

Healing childhood wounds as an adult naturally builds emotional resilience. You're less likely to be thrown off course by minor mishaps or harsh words, because your sense of self isn't as fragile or defensive. You may notice that you're able to pause before reacting with anger or impatience. You may sense there's more space inside for empathy and understanding, even when your child pushes every button.

Parenting from a place of healing means guiding your child and your inner child from love, rather than old pain or fear. Healing old wounds also expands your capacity for empathy, not only with your children but also with yourself and others around you.

When you understand the source of your pain and work through it, it becomes easier to recognize that everyone carries invisible baggage. You may see how your relationships shift. Conversations are more open. Apologies flow more easily. Practicing forgiveness becomes second nature as practice makes permanent.

You may see the transformative power of this process in some real-life stories. Consider a mid-life father, I'll call Freddy, who spent years estranged from his father after a childhood marked by criticism and harsh discipline. Freddy carried his bitter resentment into adulthood, feeling tense every time his child made a mistake. Freddy was quick to scold and slow to comfort.

Eventually, Freddy worked through radical forgiveness. He wrote letters expressing both anger and longing for approval. Even though Freddy never sent his letters to his father, writing them helped Freddy feel lighter and more at ease around his own family. Freddy couldn't rekindle a relationship with his father, who had died a few years earlier. Freddy could let go of the blame. He reports that he moved forward without the burden of bitterness in his heart.

Another example comes from a mother, I'll call Molly, who endured emotional neglect as a child. Molly's mother rarely hugged her or spoke kindly to her. As an adult, Molly struggled with intimacy and doubted her worthiness as a parent. Through guided visualizations, Molly imagined comforting herself as a young girl. Gradually, Molly began to offer her children more warmth than she'd received as a child. Molly described the process as "rewriting" her family's story, one kind word at a time.

Releasing old trauma may bring unexpected benefits, like improved sleep and less anxiety. Even physical health improves as stress hormones decrease and chronic tension subsides. After forgiving past hurts, parents often report feeling freer, more creative, and more willing to try new techniques at home.

Recognizing that forgiveness isn't always straightforward or linear is essential. You may revisit old wounds many times before they finally lose their sting. Fresh waves of anger or grief may ebb and flow as you grow through forgiving those early experiences. How do you find relief?

Practicing self-kindness soothes you each time a painful memory pops up. Remind yourself that forgiving doesn't mean forgetting or excusing past harm. It means you won't let it rule your present life. Seek help from a therapist, a support group, and trusted friends. Outside viewpoints may offer insights that help you transcend childhood trauma and learn from peace, rather than pain.

Even if forgiveness letters stay tucked away in a drawer and visualizations are done privately before bed, you may feel comforted by each step you take toward healing. These quiet acts ripple outward. Your child senses that you're less burdened by pain. Your partner sees how disagreements become less charged. Friendships shift as you bring a softened heart into your interactions. Love is soft yet infinitely powerful.

CREATE A QUANTUM SHIFT FROM LOW-VIBRATION ANGER TO HIGH-VIBRATION LOVE BY SAYING FOUR WORDS

Saying "I wish you love" quickly shifts the energy of an interaction from low vibrational feelings of anger, fear, jealousy, regret, or resentment to the highest vibrational feelings of joy, gratitude, authenticity, peace, and love.

No judgment. No analysis. It's a tender, sincere wish you can think or say to a person (or an animal or insect in the Buddha's tradition).

It isn't easy to say I WISH YOU LOVE when you're angry, hurt, triggered, frustrated, irritated, or envious. If you catch that harsh feeling seconds before you react, you can pause, breathe, and find the feeling beneath the initial reaction. Is it pain, or fear? Theirs and/or yours?

In that awareness, you soften your reaction, transforming the feeling into love through your wish.

I WISH YOU LOVE. When it's your first thought or your first words, everything shifts: The tone of an interaction. The energy. The emotional connection. The outcome.

The highest vibration of love always wins, since love-based actions and intentions are the most powerful vibrational force for productive change.

SAY THE FOUR WORDS TO A MIRROR EXERCISE

Look in a mirror and say to yourself, "I wish you love." How does it feel to talk to yourself like you are your own best friend? Practice this to see how four words can change your relationships and your life. Repetition activates neuroplasticity, rewiring your brain to embrace a new pathway to peace and joy.

SELECT NEW TRADITIONS THAT REDEFINE FAMILY DYNAMICS

Have you ever reflected on your childhood upbringing and wondered what to change and what to keep? Traditions are a great place to start. You can create defining traditions from everyday routines, like eating pizza on the floor or singing silly songs in the car.

Traditions give your family character. Something as simple as a weekly game night creates a fun emotional anchor. Game nights foster a sense of belonging, generate laughter, and create shared memories that last longer than any new gadget. The focus is on connecting, more than winning a game.

Some families create rituals around daily reflection, such as sharing "roses and thorns" at dinner or adding notes to a gratitude jar. Asking each person about a high and a low from their day fosters honesty and creates space for connection. Parents get a glimpse into their child's evolving inner world.

PROGRAM YOUR DREAMS TO COME TRUE WITH A PRE-SLEEP TRADITION

You will stop falling asleep to Netflix, your phone, worries, or stress when you use your final waking moments to imagine a desired reality you love for the next day. Then your subconscious mind works on it all night, guiding you to make it real during the day. How does that work?

Your brain rehearses your final waking thoughts for six to eight hours at night while you dream. Your subconscious mind cannot distinguish between real and imagined memories. When you feed it an imagined scenario you love every night before sleep, it creates neuro-pathways to make your imagined "memory" match reality.

You might imagine a joyful family breakfast sendoff or an inspired conversation with your manager about why you deserve a promotion, feeling enthusiastic gratitude as if it has already happened.

Even a young child can be guided through this pre-sleep ritual. It empowers children of all ages to focus on what they want, such as talking with a new friend or giving an excellent presentation, while feeling thankful and confident as if it has already occurred. Since emotions are energy in motion, the highest-vibrating emotion of gratitude attracts people and experiences at the highest vibration, allowing you to benefit from the emotional contagion of good vibes.

What if your imagined day doesn't unfold as you planned? You can model vulnerability with kind-hearted honesty by admitting what happened and committing to a plan to correct it, or by accepting it. If the outcome is firm, you might say, "Something better is on its way." This teaches by example how to adapt to life's curve balls and expect the best, while demonstrating how kind-hearted honesty can strengthen family ties.

Annual traditions enrich family life. Perhaps you host family picnics on the first day of spring, plant a tree on a birthday, and prepare a favorite meal on a child's special day. Traditions don't need to be big or expensive. What matters is consistency and intention. Silly traditions, such as pancakes for dinner on New Year's Eve or building a blanket fort on the first snow day, offer simple pleasures and joyful anticipation. They may become rituals that children carry into adulthood. Such traditions unify families and provide emotional anchors that ground you during hectic or challenging times.

CLARIFY WHAT IT MEANS TO BELONG TO YOUR FAMILY

Some families go a step further with "Family Branding." This isn't about marketing, but clarifying what membership in your family means.

Sitting down together to write a family code, guiding principles, or even a motto can make your core values visible and actionable. Mottos may be written out and displayed, or repeated in conversation. "We stick together." "Our word is our bond." "It's all about growth." Family mottos reveal what it means to belong.

You can further develop this process by drafting a family mission statement. It can be brief. The best ones are simple, understandable by even the youngest family members, and revisited yearly or during significant changes. Consider questions like, What do we stand for? How do we treat each other? What kind of family do we want to be? A family mission statement provides clarity, guiding you in growing through challenges and celebrating good times.

Traditions can be rituals that are part of your legacy, a deliberate emotional inheritance for your children. Following through on rituals, honoring shared values, and keeping promises around special nights teaches children what love looks like in practice. Missed nights or tired evenings are inevitable. What matters is the overall pattern of reliable love and unconditional connection.

CREATE A LEGACY OF LOVE EXERCISE

Create your legacy of love moment by moment with hugs before school, apologies after arguments, shared laughter, encouragement during setbacks, loving kindness, and tender honesty in interactions. Weaving loving traditions into a child's daily life shapes the adult and parent they will become.

Traditions also help repair after conflict. Returning to a favorite family ritual eases tension and signals that, despite arguments or missteps, you still come together as a family. Rituals remind everyone that belonging is unconditional.

How do you start a family tradition? Pick one tradition, such as a game night, a gratitude jar, or an evening walk, and commit to it for a month.

How do you ensure that your tradition appeals to the whole family?

BRAINSTORM TRADITIONS AND BRAND YOUR FAMILY AS A TEAM EXERCISE

Schedule an hour when you brainstorm ideas as a family. Use these prompts to write down ideas:

- What do we already do that feels special?
- What new tradition would you like to start?
- What is one value we want our family to be known for?
- Can we come up with a simple motto that fits us?

Mix and match ideas until everyone agrees on one tradition and one value statement. Post the winning answers on the fridge or a chalkboard as reminders of your family's unique journey.

Be open to trying new rituals and letting go of those that no longer serve you. Building traditions is an ongoing process that shapes your family's emotional culture and keeps you feeling close to one another at each stage of life.

Next, you'll see how lasting change takes root and positive cycles endure.

CHAPTER 10
SELECT LONG-TERM STRATEGIES FOR LASTING CHANGE

DEVELOP EMOTIONAL RESILIENCE AS A FAMILY: RECOVERING FROM SETBACKS

IMAGINE a lightning strike knocks out power, cell phone, and internet service an hour before family and friends are due for dinner. You can't call it off or cook the feast you'd planned. Instead of throwing a tantrum, you take a breath. You rally your children to find foods you can serve without cooking. Their finger food menu triggers laughs and makes cleanup a breeze.

This is a family's emotional resilience in action. It's the ability to adapt to setbacks and move forward with optimism, while facing any challenge as a team.

A family's emotional resilience is a skill that's developed by repeatedly responding effectively to life's challenges, such as losing a job, receiving a tough diagnosis, or relocating to a stressful new environment.

As a parent, resilience means maintaining your balance while facing disappointment, learning from experience, and keeping an optimistic sense of humor alive for your family. This skill helps you cope with unwelcome surprises without succumbing to dark moods. Instead, you bounce back with renewed energy, lighting a path for your child to follow.

Think of resilient parents as emotional rubber bands. They stretch under pressure and then return to their original relaxed shape. This flexibility is key because parenting is unpredictable. **Resilience** doesn't ignore hardship. It identifies feelings about the challenge and finds a constructive way forward. **Optimism** is essential. It's not pretending everything's fine. It's trusting that challenges are opportunities to learn and find solutions that promote growth.

Cultivating resilience is a lifelong process that can be strengthened day after day. Positive self-talk is a simple yet powerful tool that builds resilient optimism. When you catch yourself thinking, "I'm failing at this," try replacing it with, "I'm doing my best right now." This shift changes your stress response, restores balance, and creates good vibrations that are contagious.

Practicing gratitude rewires your brain from a state of surviving to one of thriving. Even during chaos, you can boost your outlook by taking a moment to name three things you're grateful for, such as coffee, your child's laugh, or surviving Monday. Positive affirmations ("I am patient." "We will get through this together.") build inner strength and confidence over time.

Being resilient helps you manage major life events. It also helps with everyday parenting, such as handling sibling arguments or school stress, with more patience. When you're resilient, you're modeling healthy coping for your children. They watch how you recover from losing your temper, how you rise again after a fall. They view problems as a natural part of life, rather than insurmountable obstacles. A family motto like, "We find a solution in every problem," reminds children and parents to see the silver linings in dark clouds.

Consider a resilience story from a young woman whose family had to relocate after her partner lost his job. Her children struggled with leaving friends, and she was overwhelmed. She started small. She encouraged open discussions about feelings, shared positive affirmations at bedtime, and kept a family gratitude jar. She let her children witness her working through frustration. She also included them in exploring their new town and building routines. Months later, the family had adjusted. Her children made new friends and even began to look forward to their weekly "Friday night adventure walks." Her willingness to bounce back didn't erase the pain. Yet it did help her move forward and make recovery possible. She set a lasting example for her children to follow.

REWIRE YOUR BRAIN WITH RESILIENCE EXERCISE

An angry outburst over a setback doesn't just wreck your mood; it also rewires your brain to be more reactive and impulsive. Every time you pause and breathe, instead of venting rage, you rewire your brain to build pathways toward calm, clarity, and kindness. You're steering feelings, not stuffing them. You're gaining power, not losing it, by pausing and breathing to stay calm in the face of a setback.

Journal Into Resilience

Write down a recent setback (big or small) that threw you off track. List two things you did well. "I resisted yelling at my son" counts. Add one thing you're grateful for on that day. Reread these before bed to remind yourself that setbacks are surmountable, not stumbling blocks.

The more you practice recovering from frustration or disappointment, the stronger your foundation of resilience becomes. This strengthens optimism that you can bounce back from tough setbacks. You and your entire family reap the benefits for years to come. (see APA list: 9)

CELEBRATE THIS ONE THING EACH DAY TO FUEL GROWTH AND MOMENTUM

Celebrate everyday wins to promote growth. Parenting is a marathon of mini efforts. Significant victories may be rare, but mini victories are abundant throughout each day.

You might solve a tantrum before your coffee cools. You launch your family into their day with a smile on your face and theirs. These moments may seem minor at the time, but they are the stepping stones of growth for you and your family. Growth promotes more growth when you acknowledge it. How?

CREATE RITUALS OF APPRECIATION TO ACKNOWLEDGE GROWTH

Set up a family "achievement wall." When someone in the family does something they're proud of, like finishing homework without reminders, helping a sibling, or even showing patience instead of lashing out, ask them to write it down on a sticky note and add it to the wall. Over time, this collage grows into visual reminders of progress. You can also establish a reward system for achieving both personal and shared goals. Rewards don't have to be elaborate. A family movie night, extra bedtime stories, or a special lunch on Saturday can help a child and their parents feel seen and valued for the effort. This is how you reinforce the fact that progress and kindness are noticed and valued.

What changes when families pay attention to everyday wins? One family set aside Friday evenings for "Gratitude night." Each person shared one thing they did well that week and one thing they appreciated about someone else in the room. At first, it felt awkward. Children shrugged. Parents hesitated. By the second month, everyone eagerly anticipated it. Then a shift happened. Siblings started noticing each other's good choices, like helping clean up or sharing toys, and pointed them out without being prompted. What you focus on grows. Expressing gratitude produces feel-good brain chemicals. Focusing on being part of the same team builds camaraderie.

Look for everyday wins to celebrate. When your child manages bedtime without arguments or tries broccoli for the first time, these are wins. When you resist yelling after a long day, or when you remember to breathe before reacting, give yourself credit. Acknowledging wins builds momentum. It's a reminder that change happens, one forward step at a time.

Celebrating everyday wins creates a ripple effect. Sharing in each other's victories fosters self-worth, encourages perseverance, and builds warmth that helps you feel connected, even in chaotic moments. (see APA list: 33)

TEACH EMOTIONAL INTELLIGENCE AS A FAMILY EXERCISES

Developing emotional intelligence as a family is like planting a garden together. Everyone adds something, and the results grow richer with time. When you focus on learning these skills as a team, you open the door to a greater understanding, increased patience, and a stronger connection.

As you teach a child to name feelings, you develop a shared vocabulary and learn how to spot each other's trigger signals. You don't wonder if your partner is worn out or your child is anxious if you tune into cues and respond with empathy. This habit helps your family handle conflict and turn blow-ups into opportunities for genuine connection and growth as you identify the feelings beneath the blow-ups.

When everyone in the house recognizes words like "frustrated," "overwhelmed," "nervous," and "afraid," conversations shift from blame to curiosity about what triggers tense feelings. As you manage anger with love using the skills you're learning now, you'll make it a family practice to activate triggers for more joy, peace, gratitude, and love.

Learning Turns Into Play with "Family Emotion Charades". Each person acts out a feeling (with no words), and the rest guess the feeling. You'll see how creative miming breaks the tension as you speak without words and read body language more effectively.

Creating an "Emotion Wheel" together can be a fun family activity. Cut out a circle from cardboard, divide it into slices, and write or draw each section with a different feeling, such as sad, mad, scared, embarrassed, or excited, delighted, happy, thankful. Hang it up where anyone can point to how they feel without needing to explain it out loud. This tool makes it easier for a less verbal child to share what's going on inside.

Discussing what you're learning together as a family makes it stick.
Start having regular family meetings that spark anticipation as you
share some highs and lows of a week, perhaps accompanied by choco-
late or pizza.

**Leaning into these practices as a family helps resolve issues and
build harmony. How?** Instead of separating children in a heated argument, try guiding each child to listen and repeat back what their
brother or sister is saying and feeling. Use the Emotion Wheel as a
prompt, if desired.

Fights don't vanish overnight, but each child starts feeling seen, heard,
and respected, even during disagreements. Parents feel less like
referees and more like guides. Over months, you hear more laughter
and feel more peace at home. And conflicts become learning opportunities, rather than battlefields.

Learning emotional intelligence as a family won't give you the correct
answer to every issue. It will support each of you through difficult
moments and remind you to celebrate progress as it unfolds. Each
honest interaction, each small step toward knowing and being known,
strengthens family bonds.

FUTURE-PROOF YOUR PARENTING STRATEGIES

Have you heard the saying, "If you're not growing, you're dying"?
Resilient parenting asks you to grow with each curveball life throws
you. The goal is to stay open to learning, growing, and adapting to the
issues that arise each day and in each stage of life.

Because you're reading this, it's clear you already care about doing
things better. Despite the desire for positive change, we have a mental
muscle memory that makes it easy to fall back into old habits, especially when we're tired or overwhelmed. What's an antidote?

MAKE THREE THINGS PART OF YOUR ROUTINE FOR A LIFE YOU LOVE: COMMIT TO LIFELONG LEARNING, COMMUNITY, AND CONNECTION

That may be as simple as reading an article with insights that help manage a major family transition, or listening to a parenting podcast on your commute. Podcasts like "Unruffled" with Janet Lansbury or "Raising Good Humans" with Dr. Aliza Pressman are packed with real stories and expert advice you can use right away. If you're a more visual learner, you'll find that webinars and short videos break down complex topics, such as supporting anxious kids, without demanding hours of study.

Sorrows shared are halved. Joys shared are doubled. This proverb is true for the joys of lifelong learning. Faith groups and online communities on Facebook and Reddit can double the joys by bringing parents together to share stories and swap solutions.

What does the science say? Research shows that social support not only feels good, but it also changes the brain. Supportive relationships increase neuroplasticity in brain regions that help you recover from trauma and adapt to stress. This helps your brain transition out of fight-or-flight mode more quickly, allowing for clearer thinking.

In brain scans, people with strong support networks show healthier white matter pathways -- the wiring that lets brain regions talk to each other and adjust to life changes. In the presence of a trusted person, the amygdala's danger alerts quiet down, making it easier for the prefrontal cortex to improve focus and decision-making skills. Having people you can count on literally reshapes your brain and nudges your nervous system toward resilience. (see APA list: 73)

What if you seek a more in-depth exploration? Online courses on websites like Leaply, Gaia, MindValley, Coursera, Udemy, and edX offer classes designed by universities and experts.

Topics cover a wide range, from early childhood brain science to adolescent behavior to quantum tools for productive change at any age. By taking online courses, parents who want practical tools and new perspectives can easily fit learning into busy lives.

It's never too late to learn something new and reset old patterns with guidance from parenting resources like "Starting Fresh" by Dr. Gabor Maté and Daniel Maté. They focus on repairing and nurturing relationships between parents and children, even when the kids are adults ("HELLO AGAIN," n.d.). Their approach is grounded in both science and real-life experience, offering a roadmap for families who want to stay connected through all stages of life.

You may enjoy reading helpful books. Titles like **"Parenting from the Inside Out" by Dr. Daniel Siegel, "How to Talk So Kids Will Listen & Listen So Kids Will Talk" by Adele Faber and Elaine Mazlish, and "Talking Respectfully to Your Children" by The American Montessori Society** have stood the test of time. These books explain why specific strategies work, making it easy to adapt them for your family.

When you make learning an ongoing part of parenting, you show your children that growth is a lifelong adventure. You teach by example that a failure can be a valuable source of feedback and an invitation to grow. This mindset is a gift, not just for your parenting, but also for future generations, as your children grow up and raise families, teaching them by example the love skills that are practiced until they become a habit.

RETRAIN YOUR BRAIN BEFORE IT SABOTAGES YOUR PRACTICE AND LIMITS YOUR RESULTS

How can your brain hinder your ability to manage anger with love? If your brain is stuck in a state of stress and survival mode, it will often choose a known hell over an unknown heaven. Why?

Your brain's primary function is to keep you alive -- not happy or fulfilled, but safe. A brain that's stuck in survival mode has been trained to see anger and stressful emotions as the safe, status quo. So the amygdala flags anything new as unsafe or deadly, even if it's healthy for you.

If the amygdala sabotages your new practice of managing anger with love, it's not a personality flaw. It's a neural loop. That's good news because a neural loop can be rewired with consistency, safety, and support.

"Neurons that fire together rewire together," says Hebb's Law. Consistently practicing these techniques until they become a permanent habit rewires neurons and retrains your brain to feel safe and at peace in its natural state, replacing its default state of stress with one of calm and peace. (see APA List: 89) How long do you practice this process to see results?

Shifting from a stressed, survival state to one of peaceful calm can happen quickly. Within weeks, new thoughts, emotions, and behaviors can start firing together more often, giving you glimpses of a new version of you who manages anger with love and raises a caring, confident, emotionally intelligent child in a happy relationship. Yet, permanently changing the Neural Map takes more time to solidify.

What does the science say? You may form a new thought or behavior habit through a couple of months of consistent repetition. For an enduring transformation and an identity-level rewiring, it may require 6 months to more than a year of consistent practice, repetition, reinforcement, and evidence of progress. Your brain needs this much proof that your new way of being is safe, before it permanently rewires the identity you're rehearsing, to become who you truly are.

Science also says that your brain's plasticity needs your consistent support by getting enough sleep to consolidate neural connections, by getting regular exercise to increase its BDNF--a protein that promotes the growth of neurons and synapses, by eating foods rich in Omega-3 fatty acids that support brain plasticity, and by reducing levels of stress and cortisol that hinder brain plasticity. Increasing your motivation and practicing new skills here can also help jumpstart the formation of new neural pathways that support a permanent transformation.

Some people give up before their miracle transformation becomes their new normal. Unlike you, they may not realize that a permanent transformation is inevitable when you consistently train your brain daily and celebrate each day's wins to encourage more of them. If you fall in love with this process, you'll be excited to try something new to bring out the best in yourself and become the best parent (and partner) you can be.

Remember: Until you fulfill six months of safe, enthusiastic repetition, practicing new techniques that develop new skills you love, the subconscious resists change, even productive change. Why? Because its job is to keep you "safe" by maintaining the familiar status quo. Will you fall in love with the process? It will love you back by making your brain feel safe and calm, as its new natural state.

ENGAGE YOUR SUBCONSCIOUS MIND TO SCULPT YOUR BEST FUTURE

Your other-than-conscious mind doesn't differentiate between a vividly imagined win and a real-life win. When you mentally rehearse how you respond to stressful triggers and give thanks for imagined (and real) wins as you do in exercises here, you train your subconscious mind to sculpt your best future results.

Adhering to this practice effectively improves the performance of pro athletes. For example, a pro golfer may vividly imagine playing each hole of a course before a tournament, so it feels easier to play it the "second" time on the actual course.

You're about to see how to entice your subconscious mind to work for you, instead of against you, as you practice exercises in past-tense writing about future events.

STOP CHASING THE GOAL AND EXPERIENCE THE WIN NOW: MENTAL TIME TRAVEL JOURNALING

Research on mental time travel shows that when you vividly imagine a future event, your brain processes it in much the same way as when you recall a past event. Mental time travel journaling, also known as journaling future events in the past tense, leverages this brain mechanism in your daily practice of managing anger with love.

Most people journal about what they want to happen. "I want to stop yelling and stop making my child cry." Desiring the win keeps it in the future and out of reach. Your brain stores it as wishful thinking that feels like a distant dream.

Suppose, in contrast, that you journal about your future self in the past tense, celebrating a win as if it already happened. "I love how I paused to calm down. I'm so thankful I didn't yell or make my child cry." Your past-tense recollection of a win, as if it already happened, combined with energized emotions of love and gratitude, makes the win feel real. So your brain stores it like a real memory by activating the same neural networks in the hippocampus and prefrontal cortex that encode memories. Now, you'll be able to take action on this knowledge.

BEGIN PAST-TENSE JOURNALING ABOUT FUTURE EVENTS EXERCISE

List a new topic, **Past-Tense Journaling,** in your **Manage Anger With Love Journal.** Write in the past tense for 5 minutes a day, as if you're journaling about a day last week. Describe your goal and your win in the past tense, as if you're celebrating the win that already occurred. Be sure to write in the past tense. Write what you experienced in your senses, noting what you saw, heard, touched, and how you felt about it. Write a small moment in big, loving detail. Write so it feels like you're remembering an actual event and the wonderful feelings it stirred in you, instead of imagining this in the future.

Remember, your subconscious mind accepts what you impress upon it with energized feelings and daily repetition. Past-tense journaling does both.

How does your subconscious mind interpret your past-tense journaling? It receives your past-tense recollection of what you already accomplished as information about who you are, not who you hope to become. You attract what you are, not what you want to become, according to the law of attraction.

When you write in the past tense about the joy and gratitude you felt in fulfilling your goal as if you're recalling a memory, your identity shifts, since identity is significantly built from memories. You are who you are because of your unique memories of real experiences, along with your vividly imagined experiences that your brain stores as memories.

WRITE YOUR NEW YEAR'S GOALS BACKWARDS FOR A NEW YEAR YOU LOVE

I was introduced to the benefits of past-tense goal writing by a mentor, Raymond Aaron. A business coach and a New York Times Bestselling Author of **Chicken Soup For The Canadian Soul,** Raymond explains how to write New Year's Goals Backwards as if already achieved in his book, **Double Your Income Doing What You Love.** (see APA list: 90, where you may download a digital copy of Raymond's book as his gift to parents who manage anger with love.)

My New Year's Letter To Myself: I look forward to my annual tradition of writing my New Year's Goals Backwards in a letter to myself that I write on New Year's Day. Then I read it 12 months later, on New Year's Eve, always happy to celebrate how many actual wins I experienced that year.

Raymond Aaron says that the act of writing your top goals in the past tense as if already accomplished makes some successes feel effortless, as if achieved "Automagically." How? By planting the seed in your brain that you already were successful in achieving a success once, it makes it easier to achieve again. This has proven to be true for me, each time I take the steps that I share with you now.

WRITE YOUR NEW YEAR'S GOALS BACKWARDS, SCULPTING A NEW YEAR YOU LOVE EXERCISE

1. Gather a sheet of stationery, a pen, and an envelope. In the upper right corner of your stationery or plain sheet of paper, write "New Year's Eve, December 31, (write the year ahead of you.)"
2. Record your name, possibly writing your endearing nickname that makes you smile. "Dear (write your name)"

3. Imagine the New Year is ending tonight. It's New Year's Eve. You're looking back on the last 12 months and congratulating yourself for your excellent wins and great progress you made this past year. This mental time travel on New Year's Day (or any day you write your first letter) takes you to the future (this New Year's Eve), so you can write in the past tense about your best wins and successes you achieved since New Year's Day.

4. Prepare to write your letter to yourself by choosing your top three to six goals that you're most proud of fulfilling in the past year. You'll call them successes or wins, and write them in past tense, telling your brain that you already achieved them. List the skills you enjoyed developing and the techniques you enjoyed using as you created your wins and successes. If you're celebrating wins in managing anger with love, check the Table of Contents to choose your favorites.

5. Link each chosen goal to the love(s) it supported, so you know your reason that you did this. Be sure to explain in your letter how the power of love fueled your achievements.

6. Have some fun celebrating your wonderful wins and successes in the past year, as you write the letter to yourself in the past tense, energizing your writing with love, joy, and gratitude. Be sure to mention the issues you overcame. "Some wins were challenging, requiring daily practice in developing new skills including __________________________________." "I'm thankful I stuck with this, and I love the results I experienced, including __________________________."

1. Express heartfelt thanks to yourself for all your enthusiastic efforts and actions that scattered joy and restored calm in you and your loved ones in the last year.

2. Close by writing four powerful words to yourself, "I wish you love." Then sign your name.

3. Seal your letter in an envelope. Write a note on the front: "Dear (Your Name). Read this letter as you celebrate New Year's Eve this year." Store your letter in a place where it's easily retrieved on New Year's Eve.

4. Remember, since you actually wrote this letter on New Year's Day (or the present date while doing this exercise) be sure to celebrate by doing something you love.

5. Make this an annual tradition, possibly one you teach to your child. Store all your New Year's Letters to yourself together. Enjoy re-reading them each year to celebrate your wins, your progress, and the wonders of you.

EMBRACE WABI SABI IN YOUR PARENTING JOURNEY

Perfection is a myth for parents. In daily life, the more you strive for perfection, the more you feel you're falling short. Each parent may recall memories of moments when kindness slips and patience runs thin.

You can't change the past. You can reframe your view of it with the help of the concept of "Wabi Sabi." It's a Japanese tradition that celebrates the beauty in the "perfectly imperfect." The Amish sew an imperfect square into each handmade quilt, much like the Wabi Sabi aesthetic.

How does the notion of "perfect imperfection" add unique beauty to life? Wabi Sabi inspired me to release guilt over mistakes by reframing the concept of mistakes with this viewpoint. "There are no mistakes. There are only choices with lessons attached like a bow. Learn the lessons, so you don't have to repeat them. Take new actions inspired by the lessons, because it's all about growth."

What does the science say about mistakes? The brain is wired to spot errors in less than a second, thanks to its **Error Related Negativity (ERN),** which warns us to pay attention. You can face ERN in one of two ways:

You can hold the error in your memory and get stuck replaying it repeatedly while blaming yourself for it. Or you can process the error by reframing it, finding its lesson, adapting, and moving forward. How?

TRAIN YOUR BRAIN TO STOP REPLAYING MISTAKES AND LEARN FROM THEM IN 3 STEPS:

1. The instant you recognize an error, pause and label it. This activates the prefrontal cortex to calm the emotional reaction. Think, "I criticized your mother because I was mad at her. This hurts you, which is the last thing I want to do."
2. Make a minor correction in your thoughts or actions right away. This trains your brain to link an error with an adaptive action. Say, "I'm sorry I said something mean about your mom. This hurts you, so I won't do it again. She loves you so much. And so do I."
3. Reframe the error with self-compassion and positive correction, instead of blame or criticism. Think, "I say mean things when I feel ignored, and this hurts our child. I'll make up for it by finding five good things to say about her today." Instead of, "I'm a big jerk who always screws up." (see APA list: 85 - 88)

Suppose you accept yourself as a perfectly imperfect human who's raising other perfectly imperfect humans. In that case, you break free from old habits of self-judgment. You create space to be kind to yourself. Embracing self-kindness isn't a buzzword. It's a practice that becomes second nature through repetition.

What if you catch your inner critic calling you a horrible parent after an angry outburst? You send your critic on vacation. You respond like you are your own best friend. "That was tough, yet I did my best. I can grow from this."

As you model emotional honesty and personal growth for your child, you inspire them to follow your lead and celebrate the perfectly imperfect beauty of growth in everyday life, day after day.

CONCLUSION

Thank you for sticking with me and trying out our science-backed anger management tools, techniques and exercises, which work for you when you consistently put them into practice.

You picked up this book because you wanted something to change for you and your family. You wanted a little more peace, a little less yelling, and a lot more connection. Maybe you tried to heal old wounds or stop feeling like you're walking on eggshells in your own home. Whatever brought you here, I trust that you're moving forward with a lighter heart, a stronger toolkit, a new habit you love, and a sense of resilient optimism about your family.

Let's look back at the journey we've taken together. We started by shining a gentle light on anger, what it feels like in your body, where it comes from, and why it sometimes surfaces as a shout, a slammed door, or that feeling of guilt that just won't quit.

We talked honestly about triggers, old patterns, and the ripple effect that anger can have on everyone under your roof. We considered the tough stuff without getting bogged down in it.

We learned to spot old patterns, to name them, and start loosening their grip. We practiced seeing anger, not as an enemy, but as a messenger with little flags guiding our attention to old hurts that need healing.

We tried out dozens of proven techniques and tools that build positive change in ways that retrain your brain to move from a stressed, survival mode to a thriving, calm, and peaceful mode.

Cognitive Behavioral Therapy uses thought logs to help us reframe the old stories we tell ourselves that no longer serve us.

We experimented with energy-clearing exercises, such as tapping, grounding, deep breathing, vagus nerve resetting, and even a bit of quantum jumping, to help release anger that resides in your mind and your body.

We learned how to protect our family against sneaky, toxic threats in our food, water, thinking habits and relationships.

We explored age-specific strategies for toddlers, pre-teens, and teens, as each stage brings new joys and challenges. We reviewed clinical evidence that challenges the belief that physical punishment improves behavior, and we practiced positive discipline, established new communication rituals, and learned how to redirect a meltdown (yours and your child's) away from conflict into a chance for connection.

We explored the power of empathy, honest apologies, and the transformative magic of active listening. We began to see how a little effort, such as taking a few deep breaths, practicing a bedtime gratitude ritual, and holding a family meeting, can shift the entire climate in your home.

We began to note our progress and see ourselves with more kindness. We reflected on the unique legacy each of us inherits from our parents —the good, the hard, the parts to keep, and the parts to leave behind. We faced guilt and practiced forgiveness and self-compassion.

We learned how the massive power of Emotional Contagion can work for us or against us, and how breaking old cycles is about noticing, pausing, and choosing a better path, day after day.

Have you noticed some changes already? Maybe you catch yourself before you yell. You might apologize a little sooner. Perhaps you carve out ten minutes for yourself and see how your lifted mood ripples through the family. Your child now puts words to their feelings, and your partner notices a softer tone in your voice. These aren't small wins. They're seeds of transformation.

Let's hold onto the big takeaways. Self-awareness is your anchor, letting you notice what's happening inside before it spills out. Empathy is your bridge that helps you connect with your child, even when you don't understand or agree with them. Honest, kind-hearted communication is your family's safety net.

It's not just what you say, it's also how you listen, apologize, and come back together after the storms.

Self-care isn't a luxury. It's the oxygen mask that you put on yourself first so that you can show up for your family.

And the community, the connections you make with other parents walking the same path, keep you grounded, inspired, and a little less alone.

This isn't a finish line. It's a turning point. It's all about growth, and growth work is an ongoing process. The tools in this book are meant to be used, not just read.

What's your most powerful tool? It's the power of choice. You've discovered how to choose thoughts and actions that work for you instead of against you, and produce your desired results. Will you continue to use these techniques, mainly when anger arises?

Consistency and repetition help real change stick. Brain science suggests practice makes permanent. Over time, the moments of calm last longer. The conflicts get easier to repair. The laughter comes back, sometimes in the middle of a mess.

Now you have a powerful toolkit complete with strategies, reflections, and rituals that are yours to use, adapt, and share.

If you're struggling, remember it takes a village. So reach out. Connect with your community through a faith group, a local meetup, or an online group of like-minded parents. Contact a friend who gets it. Parenting isn't meant to be a solo journey.

I want you to keep imagining your beautiful future and family life, falling in love with it, and giving thanks as if it's already here. What you see will be the result of taking the right actions. Picture a home where conflict is resolved with wise words and warmth, rather than shouting or harsh punishment.

Imagine your children growing up being able to name their feelings, ask for what they need, and rise again after a fall with the resilient optimism that builds the life and relationships they love.

Picture yourself, less burdened by anger and more able to be curious in a conflict, more proud of the parent you're becoming and the family you're guiding. This isn't a fantasy. It's a vision and a promise that you're already stepping into, one honest, perfectly imperfect step at a time.

Thank you for allowing me to guide this journey and share tools and techniques that help transform significant challenges into personal triumphs.

Thank you for your courage, your openness, and your willingness to grow. Your growth promotes more growth when you keep doing what works and stop doing what doesn't.

I encourage you to continue celebrating your wins, whether minor or significant. Choose to be curious in a conflict, not furious. Be kind, especially in the words you say to yourself. And when in doubt, come back to the basics. Breathe. Listen. Pause. Reflect. Connect. Repair. Love. That's how you become the parent and the partner you want to be, creating a family life you love.

I'm rooting for you, every step of the way, as you manage anger with love, raise a caring, confident child, and teach by example how to build emotional intelligence in happy relationships.

I'm thankful for you, and I wish you love,
Hadley Finch

KEEP THE LOVE ALIVE

Now you have everything you need to manage anger with love and teach by example how to raise confident, caring children in happy relationships. When you practice your favorite techniques for 30 consecutive days, they become a permanent part of your life and free you to learn from joy rather than pain.

Joys shared are doubled. The knowledge you've gained here doubles when you share the news of where other parents can learn to heal triggers and become the parents and partners they want to be now. How do you share the news?

Simply by leaving your honest opinion of this book on the link below, you'll show other parents where they can find the information they're looking for, and pass your passion forward to help more parents move from a stressed, survival brain state to a peaceful, calm state where love thrives.

I appreciate your help in sharing the wisdom that helps parents and children thrive.

>>> Please visit the link or scan the QR code to leave your review on Amazon.

https://amazon.com/review/review-your-purchases/?asin=
B0GR5F2711

REFERENCES

- *Unhealthy Parental Anger: Signs, Impact & How to Manage It* https://www.phas esvirginia.com/life-in-phases/uncovering-the-unhealthy-anger-that-affects-families
- *Unhealthy Parental Anger: Signs, Impact & How to Manage It* https://www.phas esvirginia.com/life-in-phases/uncovering-the-unhealthy-anger-that-affects-families#:~:text=Children%20may%20feel%20anxious%2C%20fearful,to%20develop%20anxiety%20and%20depression.
- *Byron Katie and Susan Stiffelman: The Work on Parenting* https://www.huffpost.com/entry/byron-katie-and-susan-stiffelman-the-work-and-parenting_b_7218478
- *Water, the Power of Positivity, and Education* https://fountainmagazine.com/all-issues/2019/issue-132-nov-dec-2019/water-the-power-of-positivity-and-education
- *Elevate Your Parenting: Boosting Your Child's EQ Through ...* https://toyfounda tion.org/genius/expert-advice/articles/elevate-your-parenting-boosting-your-childs-eq-through-play.aspx
- *17 Self-Awareness Tests, Activities & Exercises* https://positivepsychology.com/self-awareness-exercises-activities-test/
- *Providing Empathy in Parenting* https://psychiatryresource.com/articles/providing-empathy-in-parenting
- *Emotional Regulation: 5 Evidence-Based ...* https://positivepsychology.com/emotion-regulation/
- *9 Helpful CBT Skills for Anger Management* https://overcomewithus.com/cbt-therapy/9-helpful-cbt-skills-for-anger-management
- *How to Use Socratic Questioning to Challenge Cognitive Distortions* https://www.therapytrainings.com/pages/blog/using-socratic-questioning-to-challenge-cognitive-distortions
- *Neuroplasticity in response to cognitive behavior therapy ...* https://www.nature.com/articles/tp2015218
- *Applying Byron Katie's 4 Questions from 'The Work' for Parenting* https://www.tiktok.com/@mayimbialik/video/7166332845999394094?lang=en
- *Toddler tantrums: why they happen & how to deal with them* https://raisingchil dren.net.au/toddlers/behaviour/crying-tantrums/tantrums
- *Understanding feelings of anger - for 11-18 year olds* https://www.mind.org.uk/for-young-people/feelings-and-experiences/dealing-with-anger/
- *Weissbluth,MD., Marc. (1987) Healthy Sleep Habits, Happy Child.* Ballantine Books https://web.socaspot.org/index.jsp/libweb/1133749
- *The Five Love Languages of Teenagers* https://sobrief.com/books/the-five-love-languages-of-teenagers

- *Clinical EFT (Emotional Freedom Techniques) Improves* ... https://pmc.ncbi.nlm.nih.gov/articles/PMC6381429/
- *Practical applications of grounding to support health - PMC* https://pmc.ncbi.nlm.nih.gov/articles/PMC10105020/
- *The Connection Between Nutrition and Behavior in Children* https://www.kidsfirstservices.com/first-insights/the-connection-between-nutrition-and-behavior-inchildren#:~:text=A%20balanced%20diet%20rich%20in%20fruits%2C%20vegetables%2C%20whole%20grains%2C,%2C%20behavior%2C%20and%20social%20interactions.
- *Tips for Active Listening | Essentials for Parenting Toddlers* https://www.cdc.gov/parenting-toddlers/communication/active-listening.html
- *20 Empathy Statements to Show Your Kids You See Them* https://connectedfamilies.org/5-phrases-communicate-empathy-kids/
- *Family conflict* https://www.betterhealth.vic.gov.au/health/healthyliving/family-conflict
- *Why Children Need Boundaries: A Guide For Parents* https://nurturedfirst.com/toddler/setting-boundaries-guide/
- *Parental self-care and self-compassion* https://emergingminds.com.au/resources/parental-self-care-and-self-compassion/
- *How to reduce stress | UNICEF Parenting* https://www.unicef.org/parenting/mental-health/how-reduce-stress-parents
- *Parents Helping Parents* https://parentshelpingparents.org/
- *How the 80-20 Rule Can Help Busy Parents Achieve More by* ... https://levelupgameplan.com/mindful-parenting-resources/6689/how-the-80-20-rule-can-help-busy-parents-achieve-more-by-doing-less
- *Anger Management: Strategies for Parents and Grandparents* https://www.stanfordchildrens.org/en/topic/default?id=anger-management-strategies-for-parents-and-grandparents-160-45
- *Neurobiological Implications of Parent–Child Emotional* ... https://pmc.ncbi.nlm.nih.gov/articles/PMC8391119/
- *CBT for Anger: How It Works, Techniques, & Effectiveness* https://www.choosingtherapy.com/cbt-for-anger/
- *Clinical EFT (Emotional Freedom Techniques) Improves* ... https://pmc.ncbi.nlm.nih.gov/articles/PMC6381429/
- *The Past Is Present: The Impact of Your Childhood* ... https://www.zerotothree.org/resource/the-past-is-present-the-impact-of-your-childhood-experiences-on-how-you-parent-today/
- *7 Ways to Break Generational Parenting Cycles* https://www.psychedmommy.com/blog/7-ways-to-break-generational-parenting-cycles
- *Radical Forgiveness: A Revolutionary Five-Stage Process* https://radicalforgiveness.org/product/radical-forgiveness-a-revolutionary-five-stage-process/
- *Family Mission Statement: How and Why to Create One for* ... https://www.artofmanliness.com/people/family/creating-a-family-culture-how-and-why-to-create-a-family-mission-statement/
- *Resilient kids: How parental self-awareness is critical to* ... https://journals.sagepub.com/doi/10.1177/02614294241274442#:~:text=Based%20on%20Baum

rind's%20(2013)%20classifica-
tions,low%20warmth%3B%20high%20control)%20or

- *From Small Steps to Big Wins: The Importance of Celebrating* https://www.psychologytoday.com/us/blog/empower-your-mind/202406/from-small-steps-to-big-wins-the-importance-of-celebrating
- *How to Teach Emotional Intelligence to Children* https://betteringyouth.co.uk/blog/emotional-literacy-30-activities
- *HELLO AGAIN* https://www.helloagainproject.com
- *Grimanasa Revelo Herrera 1, Silvia. Leon-rojas, Jose.* (2025) *The Effect of Aerobic Exercise in Neuroplasticity, Learning, and Cognition: A Systematic Review* https://pmc.ncbi.nlm.nih.gov/articles/PMC10932589
- (Huberman, 2021) Stanford Neuroscience Institute research on physiological sigh and vagus nerve regulation.
- (Harvard Medical School, 2019)Harvard Health Publishing on the role of the vagus nerve in stress and recovery
- (PubMed Central, 2018) National Institutes of Health review on vagus nerve stimulation and health outcomes.
- (Tracey, 2002). Journal of Clinical Investigation on inflammation control via parasympathetic pathways
- Serum and plasma brain-derived neurotropic factor concentration are elevated by systemic but not local passive heating https://doi.org/10.137/journal.pone.0260775 Head-out immersion in hot water increases serum BDNF in healthy males https://pubmet.ncbi.nlm.nih.gov/29157042
- Before-bedtime passive body heating by warm shower or bath to improve sleep: A systematic review and meta-analysis https://pubmed.ncbi.nlm.nih.gov/31102877
- Recovery from sauna bathing favorable modulates cardiac autonomic nervous system https://pubmed.ncbi.nlm.nih.gov/31331560/
- Kubler-Ross, MD, Elizabeth (1969) On Death And Dying, observed the Five Stages of Grief in terminally ill patients; later applied the five stages to the broader experience of grief and loss.
- The Institute for Learning & Brain Science at ilabs.washington.edu
- The Anti-Anxiety Notebook by Therapy Notebooks. https://www.avocadodiaries.com/2021/07/the-anti-anxiety-notebook.html
- Association Between Consumption of Low- and No-Calorie Artificial Sweeteners and Cognitive Decline Neurology Journal (October 7, 2025 Issue) https://www.neurology.org/doi/10.1212/WNL.000000000021 4023Natalia Gomes Gonçalves et al. https://orcid.org/0000-0002-5253-5483
- The Modern Health Benefits of Chinese Qigong (October 29, 2024) Jun Zhang1,2*, Dubae Jeong3, Yingying Yu4, Haiying Wang5 and Chenchen Tan4 https://juniperpublishers.com/jojo/JOJO.MS.ID.555823.php#:~:text=Conclusion-,Conclusion,various%20ages%20and%20health%20conditions.
- Cognitive Reappraisal Changes Neural Processes As Detected on Brain Scans: Psychology Today Staff https://psychologytoday.com/us/basics/cognitive-reappraisal#:~:text=Strong%20emotions%20limit%20thinking%20processes,regions%20linked%20to%20arithmetic%20performance.

- Chapman, Gary D. Campbell, MD, Ross. (1997) The 5 Love Languages of Children. Moody Publishers
- McLeod, PhD. Saul (2025) Maslow's Hierarchy of Needs (August 3, 2025 updated) https://Simplypsychology.org/maslow.html
- Perlmutter, MD, David. (2015) Brain Maker. Little Brown. Chapter 3: Why Angry Guts Make for Moody and Anxious Minds.
- Your Favorite Music Can Send Your Brain Into A Pleasure Overload. https://frontiersin.org/news/2020/11/03/neurological-basis-experiencing-chills-from-music
- Auditory and reward structures reflect the pleasure of musical expectancies during naturalistic listening https://pmc.ncbi.nlm.nih.gov/articles/PMC10625409/
- Nihart AJ et al. (2025) Bioaccumulation of microplastics in decedent human brains. Nat Med. 2025; DOI:10.1038/s41591-024-03453-1.
- Microplastics Found in Human Brains: An Alarming Link to Dementia. American Medical Journal (Feb 13, 2025) https://www.emjreviews.com/en-us/amj/neurology/news/microplastics-found-in-human-brains-an-alarming-link-to-dementia/
- Vaillant, MD, George (1977). **Adaptation to Life.** A classic text on adult development based on the early findings of the Harvard Grant Study.
- Vaillant, MD, George (2002) _Aging Well_: A later book that uses the data to explain the factors separating the "happy-well" from the "sad-sick" in later life. Little Brown Spark.
- Vaillant, MD, George (2012) _Triumphs of Experience_: The Men Of The Harvard Grand Study. A comprehensive summary of the Grant Study and the men's lives into their nineties.
- Gottman, John M and DeClaire,Joan. (2002) The Relationship Cure: A 5 Step Guide to Strengthening Your Marriage, Family, and Friendships. Harmony.
- Glass, Russell. (2024) Boundaries, Priorities, and Finding Work-Life Balance (HBR Work Smart Series) Harvard Business Review
- Jargon, Julie. (2025) Wall Street Journal https://www.wsj.com/health/wellness/boys-social-isolation-warning-signs-6233628b?mod=wsjhp_columnists_pos_1 (9-22-25)
- Jargon, Julie. (2025) The Case For Snooping On Your Kid's Phone. Wall Street Journal. (7-12-2025) https://www.wsj.com/tech/personal-tech/the-case-for-snooping-on-your-kids-phone-a6a7a547?mod=article_inline
- Herrando C, Constantinides E.(2021) Emotional Contagion: A Brief Overview and Future Directions. Front Psychol. (2021 Jul 16) 12:712606. doi: 10.3389/fpsyg.2021.712606. PMID: 34335425; PMCID: PMC8322226.
- Kramer AD, Guillory JE, Hancock JT. (2014) Experimental evidence of massive-scale emotional contagion through social networks. Proc Natl Acad Sci U S A. (2014 June 17) 111(24):8788-90. doi: 10.1073/pnas . 1320040111. Epub 2014 Jun 2. PMID: 24889601; PMCID: PMC4066473.
- The Neurobiological Impact of Oxytocin in Mental Health Disorders: A Comprehensive Review
- https://pmc.ncbi.nlm.nih.gov/articles/PMC11981257/

- Association of Social Support with Brain Volume and Cognition https://jamanetwork.com/journals/jamanetworkopen/fullarticle/2783042
- Tipping, Colin. (2010) Radical Forgiveness: A Revolutionary Five-Stage Process to Heal Relationships, Let Go of Anger and Blame, and Find Peace in Any Situation. Sounds True.
- Scovel-Shinn, Florence. (1989) The Wisdom Of Florence Scovel Shinn: Four Complete Books. Simon and Schuster
- Shoab, Alia. (2025) https://www.newsweek.com/map-drinking-water-multiple-contaminants-2133662
- Sapolsky, Robert M. (1993) Why Zebras Don't Get Ulcers. Stanford University research on complaining + stress responses.
- McKewen et al. (2007) Nature Reviews Neuroscience Studies on hippocampus shrinkage under chronic cortisol.
- Lupien et al. (2009) Nature Reviews Neuroscience Research on amygdala activation + negative self-talk.
- Fox et al. (2015) Frontiers In Psychology Studies on gratitude increasing hippocampus activity and lowering cortisol.
- Zacharias, Danny. (2015) https://www.dannyzacharias.net/blog/2015/5/7/dont-spare-the-rod-recovering-the-biblical-perspective-on-disciplining-your-children#:~:text=The%20Biblical%20Rod,%22%20or%20%22shepherd%20crook.%22
- Baumeister, R.F., et al. (2001) Bad is Stronger Than Good. Review of General Psychology.
- Rozin, P., & Royzman, E. (2001) Negativity Bias, Negativity Dominance. Personality & Social Psychology Review.
- Siegle, G.J. et al. (2002) Amygdala and Hippocampal Activation in Depression. Biological Psychiatry.
- Gottman, J. (1994) What Predicts Divorce? — 5:1 positive-to-negative ratio.
- Neural correlates of error-monitoring and mindset: Back to the drawing board? https://pmc.ncbi.nlm.nih.gov/articles/PMC8318296/
- Learning from errors: Distinct neural networks for monitoring errors and maintaining corrections through repeated practice and feedback https://doi.org/10.1016/j.neuroimage.2023.120001
- Neural and behavioral dynamics of error processing under chronic stress in healthy young adults https://doi.org/10.1016/j.ijchp.2025.100561
- Calbet, Josep. Hebbs Rule With An Analogy. Psychology And Neuroscience. https://neuroquotient.com/en/pshychology-and-neuroscience-hebb-principle-rule/#:~:text=The%20Hebb's%20principle%20or%20Hebb's,and%20behaviour%20with%20neural%20networks.
- Aaron, Raymond. (2008) Double Your Income Doing What You Love. Wiley. Download your digital copy as Raymond's gift when you visit https://www.aaron.com
- Milbank, Dana. Results Of A 6-Year Study Out Of Cornell Suggests A Happiness Hack That Can Lead You Toward A Life Of Purpose. https://www.washingtonpost.com/climate-environment/2025/10/24/happiness-purpose-community-contribution/

- The Neurochemistry and Social Flow Of Singing, Bonding And Oxytocin. https://pubmed.ncbi.nlm.nih.gov/28663005
- Bergland, Christopher. (2017) Face-to-Face Connectedness, Oxytocin And Your Vagus Nerve. PsychologyToday.com https://www.psychologytoday.com/us/blog/the-athletes-way/201705/face-face-connectedness-oxytocin-and-your-vagus-nerve

Disclaimer: This content is for informational purposes only. It's important to consult a healthcare professional before making any changes to your health and wellness protocols.

CLAIM YOUR BONUSES AND CONNECT WITH OUR COMMUNITY OF RESILIENT OPTIMISTS WHO BELIEVE IN GREAT LOVE

Explore expert love tips for happy relationships shared since 2009 on our blog at HappySexyLove.com. Also on our blog, click **Parents Manage Anger With Love JOURNAL** to download the journaling topic list that guides your growth through journaling exercises.

Claim a Gift Audiobook featuring dozens of my favorite radio interviews with America's premier relationship success and love experts: HappySexyLoveInRomanticRelationships.com.

Download a digital copy of my breakup survival book. Visit: 3HourBreakupSurvival.com (gift code: heartbreak2happiness)

Check out my novel, **TRIBE OF BLONDES**, named not for a hair color but for resilient optimists who believe in great love. Visit My Book

Listen to my novel soundtrack – a "Soulgrass" country and bluegrass album of songs that start with lost love and end in the fire of love. Visit our blog: HappySexyLove.com Click: Love Songs.

All song lyrics evolved while I did my "morning pages" exercise that you're exploring in **ANGER MANAGEMENT FOR PARENTS** Who

Manage Anger With Love. Are you curious how these exercises will inspire you and your family?

Tap away stress with a 5-day gift pass to a 10-day tapping course led by tapping foundation founder, Nick Ortner. Visit http://bit.ly/3JimrAe

Download a digital copy of bestselling author, Raymond Aaron's book, **Double Your Income Doing What You Love.** It's Raymond's gift to parents who manage anger with love. Visit https://aaron.com/home